The Atlantic Slave Trade

PROBLEMS IN WORLD
HISTORY SERIES

The Atlantic Slave Trade

Third Edition

Edited and with an introduction by

David Northrup
Boston College

WADSWORTH
CENGAGE Learning™

Australia • Brazil • Japan • Korea • Mexico • Singapore • Spain • United Kingdom • United States

WADSWORTH
CENGAGE Learning™

The Atlantic Slave Trade,
Third Edition

David Northrup

Senior Publisher: Suzanne Jeans

Senior Acquisitions Editor:
Nancy Blaine

Senior Development Manager:
Jeffrey Greene

Assistant Editor: Lauren Floyd

Editorial Assistant:
Emma Goehring

Senior Media Editor:
Lisa Ciccolo

Marketing Manager:
Katherine Bates

Marketing Coordinator:
Lorreen Pelletier

Marketing Communications
Manager: Christine Dobberpuhl

Senior Content Project
Manager: Shelley Dickerson

Senior Art Director:
Cate Rickard Barr

Print Buyer: Paula Vang

Permissions Editor: Bob Kauser

Production Service:
Pre-PressPMG

Photo Manager: Jennifer Meyer
Dare

Cover Image: North Wind
Picture Archives

Compositor: Pre-PressPMG

For product information and
technology assistance, contact us at **Cengage Learning
Customer & Sales Support, 1-800-354-9706**

For permission to use material from this text or product,
submit all requests online at **cengage.com/permissions**
Further permissions questions can be emailed to
permissionrequest@cengage.com

Library of Congress Control Number: 2009932938

ISBN-13: 978-0-618-64356-1

ISBN-10: 0-618-64356-7

Wadsworth
20 Channel Center Street
Boston, MA 02210
USA

Cengage Learning is a leading provider of customized learning solutions with office locations around the globe, including Singapore, the United Kingdom, Australia, Mexico, Brazil, and Japan. Locate your local office at **www.cengage.com/global.**

Cengage Learning products are represented in Canada by Nelson Education, Ltd.

To learn more about Wadsworth, visit
www.cengage.com/wadsworth

Purchase any of our products at your local college store or at our preferred online store **www.ichapters.com**

Printed in the United States of America
1 2 3 4 5 6 7 13 12 11 10 09

Contents

VI Africans and Abolition   147

Preface

Since the first edition of this anthology appeared in 1994, the slave trade from Africa to the Americas has continued to be a subject of lively new research and reinterpretation. Recent studies have explored new issues, proposed new answers to old questions, and provided the basis for a much more precise understanding of this important and sensitive subject. The third edition of *The Atlantic Slave Trade* brings together a representative sample of this new scholarly writing by historians from both sides of the Atlantic, including many that are new to this work. It places the modern works in a larger historical context by including some records from contemporary eyewitnesses, both black and white, along with selections from influential older histories of the Atlantic slave trade.

Part I probes the reasons why Africans became the dominant labor force for European settlers in some parts of the Americas. Part II explores the African systems that produced and managed the flow of slaves to the coast, and Part III looks at the European voyages that carried these captives to the Americas. Parts IV and V present a sample of the interpretations that have been offered of the consequences of the slave trade in Africa, in Europe, and in the Americas. Finally, Part VI examines the forces that brought the trade to an end.

As a volume in the Problems in World History series, *The Atlantic Slave Trade* treats a subject whose scope extends beyond the limits of any single continent or nation. During the four centuries of the Atlantic slave trade, Europeans (and European-Americans) transported Africans to the Caribbean, South America, and North America, establishing indelible links among these once separated lands. For this reason this volume can be a useful addition to courses treating either global interactions or the separate histories of the lands the slave trade affected.

I am grateful for the constructive comments of the following historians, who reviewed the table of contents at various stages: Lisa Lindsay, University of North Carolina; DeeAnna Manning, University of Nebraska-Lincoln; G. Ugo Nwokeji, University of Connecticut; David Owusu-Ansah, James Madison University; and Timothy J. Shannon, Gettysburg College.

D. N.

Introduction

Slavery and the slave trade began long before the first enslaved Africans crossed the Atlantic in the sixteenth century. Harvard sociologist Orlando Patterson opens his great comparative study, *Slavery and Social Death*, with the observation that slavery "has existed from before the dawn of human society . . . in the most primitive societies and in the most civilized. There is no region on earth that has not at some time harbored the institution. Probably there is no group of people whose ancestors were not at one time slaves or slaveholders." Even the plantation system, so central to the slave experience in the Americas, first appeared in the Mediterranean world. Prior to the fifteenth century, most enslaved persons were not Africans.

Yet the Atlantic commerce in African slaves has attracted more attention than any other slave trade because of the magnitude of its historical legacies. First, it brought many millions of Africans to the Americas (four times the number of European immigrants who settled there down to about 1820), leaving a permanent cultural and genetic imprint on many parts of the New World. Second, the creation of slave labor systems in the New World was associated with the first phase of European expansion and the rise of capitalism. Third, the end of the slave trade was the subject of a massive abolitionist campaign that scholars widely have seen as one of the great turning points in Western moral consciousness. Finally, the Atlantic slave trade has been seen not only as affecting Africa during the four centuries of its existence but also as leading to the later European takeover of the continent and causing its present-day underdevelopment.

African slaves played important roles in the conquest and economic development of the Americas from the early days of Spanish colonization. They were also the base upon which Portuguese Brazil became the world's major sugar producer in the early seventeenth century. However, the Atlantic slave trade's greatest importance in the development of the New World and a vital South Atlantic economy dates from the mid-seventeenth century, when Dutch capitalists transferred the sugar plantation economy from northern Brazil to the West Indies. Wresting Caribbean islands from Spanish control, the English established sugar plantations in Barbados and Jamaica, the French in Saint Domingue (modern Haiti), and other nations elsewhere, significantly increasing the demand for slave labor.

The Atlantic slave trade expanded rapidly because it was put on a firm business footing. Most of the growing number of slaving ships crossing the Atlantic belonged to European trading companies that had established permanent outposts and other contacts along the African coast. Large sums of capital from private investors financed the great trading circuit that ran from Europe to Africa, from Africa to the Americas, and back to Europe. European factories turned out special guns and other goods that were used to buy slaves in Africa, supplemented by cotton textiles brought from India and rum and tobacco from the Americas. European governments protected these profitable commercial empires from outside competition.

The search for slaves opened more and more parts of Africa to the trade. Angola and the adjoining coast north of the Congo River composed the most important trading area overall, whereas the infamous Slave Coast and the Bight of Biafra on the Gulf of Guinea dominated slave trade north of the equator during the century after 1740. From the late eighteenth century, even far distant parts of southeastern Africa were tapped for the Atlantic slave trade. Slaving became a business in Africa, too. In some places networks of slave markets fed victims to the coast, where they were sold by professional African traders and by powerful rulers, who successfully drove up the prices and fees paid by European slave dealers. Yet at its base the trade rested on violence that spread farther and farther inland from the coast. Ultimately, most of those sold into slavery were the victims of war, kidnapping, famine, debt, and social oppression.

By 1700 the West Indies had surpassed Brazil in sugar production, but Portugal's giant South American colony retained its importance as the major destination of the transatlantic slave trade for two more centuries. As Brazil's sugar industry felt the impact of competition, slaves were diverted to almost every sort of job imaginable—they worked as miners, cowboys, stevedores, and factory laborers. In the nineteenth century, investment in new sugar plantations made Cuba a major importer of slaves. The territories that became part of the United States imported a modest share of the slave trade (fewer than the small Caribbean island of Barbados), but on the eve of emancipation, the United States had the largest slave population the Western world had ever seen.

In the eighteenth century, slavery came under mounting attack by philosophical and religious thinkers as well as by slave rebels. Antislavery societies sprang up in many Western countries. Ironically, it was in Great Britain, whose traders dominated the carrying of slaves across the Atlantic, that the largest and most influential abolitionist movement arose. Led by religious idealists—Quakers, Methodists, and evangelical Anglicans—the British abolitionist movement also gained the support of a new industrial middle class, whose members identified slavery with the outmoded political economy of the old colonial system. For both ethical and economic reasons, these people supported the abolition of the slave trade as the first step toward ending slavery.

In 1808 a new law prohibited the participation of British subjects in the Atlantic slave trade. The expiration that same year of a twenty-year ban written into the Constitution permitted the U.S. Congress to enact similar legislation with regard to American citizens. Other Western nations followed suit: the Netherlands in 1814, France in 1831, Spain (under great pressure from Great Britain) in 1835, Portugal in 1846, and Brazil in 1850. Despite these laws and the enforcement measures spearheaded by the British, the Atlantic slave trade remained vigorous as long as a strong demand for slaves existed. Only after slavery finally was outlawed in the United States, the French and Dutch colonies, and the former Spanish colonies did the last known slave ships make their crossings in 1867. Brazil and Cuba ended slavery in 1886 and 1888.

For a long time the history of the slave trade was dominated by the writings of the British abolitionists who gathered data on sailings, interviewed sailors and captains in the British slaving ports, and encouraged participants and victims to publish accounts of their experiences. Because their evidence faced close scrutiny from the vested interests in Parliament who defended the slave trade, these abolitionist accounts generally were highly accurate. However, because their intention was not the objective analysis of the operations of the slave trade but a propaganda campaign to move the hearts and minds of members of Parliament and their constituents to end the trade, they concentrated on incidents of such extreme inhumanity that even the most hardhearted would be moved to act.

Understanding of the Atlantic slave trade continues to be shaped by the abolitionist tradition, but two influential works of modern scholarship have directed attention to issues besides the trade's immorality and cruelties. *Capitalism and Slavery*, a brief and readable survey published in 1944 by the young West Indian historian Eric Williams, focused attention on the trade's economic importance. Williams, who later became prime minister of Trinidad and Tobago, argued that the slave trade was of central importance to the rise of commercial capitalism in the seventeenth and eighteenth centuries and that the end of the slave trade was linked intimately with the emergence of the new industrial capitalists, who had good economic reasons for seeking its demise. He also argued that the end of slavery had as much to do with changes in economics as with changes in ideas of morality.

The Atlantic Slave Trade: A Census, published in 1969 by historian Philip D. Curtin, profoundly altered slave trade historiography by examining a different topic. The foremost American-born specialist in the emerging field of African history and later the president of the American Historical Association, Curtin sought the answer to a simple factual question: How many slaves were transported from Africa to the Americas? His estimate, based on published sources then available, was lower than the figure commonly accepted and set off new research and controversy. The careful sifting of archival records by other scholars has improved many of Curtin's original estimates of where slaves came from, where they went, and how volumes changed over time. Scholars led by David Eltis in 2008 posted on the Internet a massive database with information on nearly 35,000 slaving voyages. Such statistical research also permits more precise assessments of the effects of the slave trade in different parts of Africa, of the profits received by different carriers, of the causes of the mortality during the Middle Passage, and of the reasons why slave populations multiplied or failed to multiply in different parts of the Americas.

Interest in the Atlantic slave trade in recent decades was stimulated not simply by new historical works. In the United States, the successes of the civil rights and black power movements sparked interest in African American history, including the slave trade and its legacy. The postwar decolonization of Africa kindled new interest in African history in African, European, and American universities, including a reexamination of the role of the slave trade in African history. Indeed, much recent writing on the Atlantic slave trade is the work of scholars who specialize in African history, and it reflects the scholarly developments in that field. In addition, the end of colonial empires in Asia, Africa, and the West Indies has generated a debate over the persistence of Western economic imperialism and the role of the Atlantic slave trade in the creation of underdevelopment and neocolonialism. Finally, historians' growing focus on the Atlantic as a proper area of study has led to lively debates about the contributions of enslaved Africans to the cultures of the New World and the importance of slavery and the slave trade in the development of Europe and the Americas.

In light of the complexities of the long history of the Atlantic slave trade and of the questions asked by modern constituencies, it is not surprising that many historical controversies remain unresolved. Still, the readings in this volume document recent advances in knowledge about the Atlantic slave trade and show how historical debates can refine our understanding of important issues.

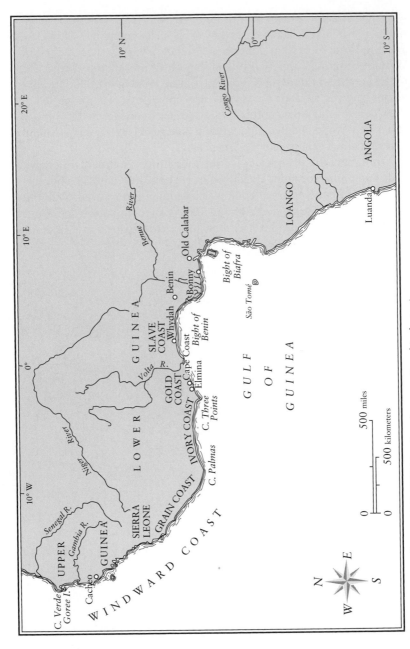

Map 1. Western Africa, c. 1640–1750 (showing places mentioned in the text).

I Why Were Africans Enslaved?

Slavery was not born of racism: rather, racism was the consequence of slavery. . . . The origin of Negro slavery was economic, not racial; it had to do not with the color of the laborer, but the cheapness of the labor.

ERIC WILLIAMS

In a profound . . . sense chattel slavery for Africans and Indians in the Americas was . . , a function of the non-slave status that Europeans considered inappropriate for themselves.

DAVID ELTIS

[A] precondition [for New World slavery] was the medieval Arab precedent of enslaving and transporting by ship or caravan enormous numbers of black Africans. . . .

DAVID BRION DAVIS

1

. . . whatever notions Europeans might have had about Africans in general, those whom the English and Dutch brought to the early colonies appeared much more like insiders and were treated as such.

LINDA M. HEYWOOD AND JOHN K. THORNTON

Eric Williams

Economics, Not Racism, as the Root of Slavery

The high level of prejudice against blacks during and after slavery might suggest that the enslavement of Africans began as the result of racism. However, more than a half-century ago, the influential West Indian historian Eric Williams forcefully argued that this was not the case. Slavery caused racism, but economic motives, not racial impulses, caused slavery. The rise of plantation slavery was tied to the development of capitalism; the capitalists' decision to import large numbers of Africans and to hold them in hereditary bondage was based on the fact that enslaved Africans were cheaper than any other available form of labor. In the West Indies and other parts of the Americas, a second cold-blooded financial calculation—that it was cheaper to import a young adult slave than to raise one born in slavery on a plantation—necessitated continuous fresh shipments of enslaved Africans.

Slavery in the Caribbean has been too narrowly identified with the Negro. A racial twist has thereby been given to what is basically an economic phenomenon. Slavery was not born of racism: rather, racism was the consequence of slavery. Unfree labor in the New World was brown, white, black, and yellow; Catholic, Protestant, and pagan.

Eric Williams, "Economics, Not Racism, as the Root of Slavery," from *Capitalism and Slavery*, pp. 7–13, 18–23, 29, 126–127, 135–136, 169–173, 187–192. Copyright © 1944 by the University of North Carolina Press, renewed 1972 by Eric Williams. New introduction by Colin A. Palmer © 1994 by the University of North Carolina Press. Reprinted by permission of the publisher, www.uncpress.unc.edu.

The first instance of slave trading and slave labor developed in the New World involved, racially, not the Negro but the Indian. The Indians rapidly succumbed to the excessive labor demanded of them, the insufficient diet, the white man's diseases, and their inability to adjust themselves to the new way of life. Accustomed to a life of liberty, their constitution and temperament were ill-adapted to the rigors of plantation slavery. As Fernando Ortíz writes: "To subject the Indian to the mines, to their monotonous, insane and severe labor, without tribal sense, without religious ritual, . . . was like taking away from him the meaning of his life. . . . It was to enslave not only his muscles but also his collective spirit." . . .

England and France, in their colonies, followed the Spanish practice of enslavement of the Indians. There was one conspicuous difference— the attempts of the Spanish Crown, however ineffective, to restrict Indian slavery to those who refused to accept Christianity and to the warlike Caribs on the specious plea that they were cannibals. From the standpoint of the British government Indian slavery, unlike later Negro slavery which involved vital imperial interests, was a purely colonial matter. . . . But Indian slavery never was extensive in the British dominions. . . .

The immediate successor of the Indian . . . was not the Negro but the poor white. These white servants included a variety of types. Some were indentured servants, so called because, before departure from the homeland, they had signed a contract, indented by law, binding them to service for a stipulated time in return for their passage. Still others, known as "redemptioners," arranged with the captain of the ship to pay for their passage on arrival or within a specified time thereafter; if they did not, they were sold by the captain to the highest bidder. Others were convicts, sent out by the deliberate policy of the home government, to serve for a specified period. . . .

A regular traffic developed in these indentured servants. Between 1654 and 1685 ten thousand sailed from Bristol alone, chiefly for the West Indies and Virginia. In 1683 white servants represented one-sixth of Virginia's population. Two thirds of the immigrants to Pennsylvania during the eighteenth century were white servants; in four years 25,000 came to Philadelphia alone. It has been estimated that more than a quarter of a million persons were of this class during the colonial period, and that they probably constituted one-half of all English immigrants, the majority going to the middle colonies.

As commercial speculation entered the picture, abuses crept in. Kidnapping was encouraged to a great degree and became a regular business in such town[s] as London and Bristol. Adults would be plied with liquor, children enticed with sweetmeats. The kidnappers were called "spirits," defined as "one that taketh upp men and women and children and sells them on a shipp to be conveyed beyond the sea." The captain of a ship trading to Jamaica would visit the Clerkenwell House of Correction, ply with drink the girls who had been imprisoned there as disorderly, and "invite" them to go to the West Indies. The temptations held out to the unwary and the credulous were so attractive that, as the mayor of Bristol complained, husbands were induced to forsake their wives, wives their husbands, and apprentices their masters, while wanted criminals found on the transport ships a refuge from the arms of the law. . . .

Convicts provided another steady source of white labor. The harsh feudal laws of England recognized three hundred capital crimes. Typical hanging offences included: picking a pocket for more than a shilling; shoplifting to the value of five shillings; stealing a horse or a sheep; poaching rabbits on a gentleman's estate. Offences for which the punishment prescribed by law was transportation comprised the stealing of cloth, burning stacks of corn, the maiming and killing of cattle, hindering customs officers in the execution of their duty, and corrupt legal practices. Proposals made in 1664 would have banished to the colonies all vagrants, rogues and idlers, petty thieves, gipsies, and loose persons frequenting unlicensed brothels. A piteous petition in 1667 prayed for transportation instead of the death sentence for a wife convicted of stealing goods valued at three shillings and four pence. In 1745 transportation was the penalty for the theft of a silver spoon and a gold watch. One year after the emancipation of the Negro slaves, transportation was the penalty for trade union activity. It is difficult to resist the conclusion that there was some connection between the law and the labor needs of the plantations, and the marvel is that so few people ended up in the colonies overseas. . . .

The political and civil disturbances in England between 1640 and 1740 augmented the supply of white servants. Political and religious nonconformists paid for their unorthodoxy by transportation, mostly to the sugar islands. Such was the fate of many of Cromwell's Irish prisoners, who were sent to the West Indies. So thoroughly was this policy pursued that an active verb was added to the English language—to "barbadoes" a person. Montserrat became largely an Irish colony, and the Irish brogue is still frequently heard today in many parts of the British West Indies. The Irish, however, were poor servants. They hated the English, were always ready to aid England's enemies, and in a revolt in the Leeward Islands in 1689 we can already see signs of that burning indignation which, according to Lecky, gave Washington some of his best soldiers. The vanquished in Cromwell's Scottish campaigns were treated like the Irish before them, and Scotsmen came to be regarded as "the general travaillers and soldiers in most foreign parts." Religious intolerance sent more workers to the plantations. In 1661 Quakers refusing to take the oath for the third time were to be transported; in 1664 transportation, to any plantation except Virginia or New England, or a fine of one hundred pounds was decreed for the third offence for persons over sixteen assembling in groups of five or more under pretence of religion. Many of Monmouth's adherents were sent to Barbados, with orders to be detained as servants for ten years. The prisoners were granted in batches to favorite courtiers, who made handsome profits from the traffic in which, it is alleged, even the Queen shared. A similar policy was resorted to after the Jacobite risings of the eighteenth century. . . .

The institution of white servitude, however, had grave disadvantages. Postlethwayt, a rigid mercantilist, argued that white laborers in colonies would tend to create rivalry with the mother country in manufacturing. Better black slaves on plantations than white servants in industry, which would encourage aspirations to independence. The supply moreover was becoming increasingly difficult, and the need of the plantations outstripped the English convictions. In addition, merchants were involved in many vexatious and costly proceedings arising from people signifying their willingness to emigrate, accepting food and clothes in advance, and then sueing for unlawful detention. Indentured servants were not forthcoming in sufficient quantities to replace those who had served their term. On the plantations, escape was easy for the white servant; less easy for the Negro who, if freed, tended, in self-defence, to stay in his locality where he was well known and less likely to be apprehended as a vagrant or runaway slave. The servant expected land at the end of his contract; the Negro, in a strange environment, conspicuous by his color and features, and ignorant of the white man's language and ways, could be kept permanently divorced from the land. Racial differences made it easier to justify and rationalize Negro slavery, to exact the mechanical obedience of a plough-ox or a cart-horse, to demand that resignation and that complete moral and intellectual subjection which alone make slave labor possible. Finally, and this was the decisive factor, the Negro slave was cheaper. The money which procured a white man's services for ten years could buy a Negro for life. As the governor of Barbados stated, the Barbadian planters found by experience that "three blacks work better and cheaper than one white man."

But the experience with white servitude had been invaluable. Kidnaping in Africa encountered no such difficulties as were encountered in England. Captains and ships had the experience of the one trade to guide them in the other. Bristol, the center of the servant trade, became one of the centers of the slave trade. Capital accumulated from the one financed the other. White servitude was the historic base upon which Negro slavery was constructed. The felon-drivers in the plantations became without effort slave-drivers. "In significant numbers," writes Professor Phillips, "the Africans were latecomers fitted into a system already developed."

Here, then, is the origin of Negro slavery. The reason was economic, not racial; it had to do not with the color of the laborer, but the cheapness of the labor. As compared with Indian and white labor, Negro slavery was eminently superior. "In each case," writes Bassett, discussing North Carolina, "it was a survival of the fittest. Both Indian slavery and white servitude were to go down before the black man's superior endurance, docility, and labor capacity." The features of the man, his hair, color and dentifrice, his "subhuman" characteristics so widely pleaded, were only the later rationalizations to justify a simple economic fact: that the colonies needed labor and resorted to Negro labor because it was cheapest and best. This was not a theory, it was a practical conclusion deduced from the personal experience of the planter. He would have gone to the moon, if necessary, for labor. Africa was nearer than the moon, nearer too than the more populous countries of India and China. But their turn was to come. . . .

Negro slavery, thus, had nothing to do with climate. Its origin can be expressed in three words: in the Caribbean, Sugar; on the mainland, Tobacco and Cotton. A change in the economic structure produced a corresponding change in the labor supply. The fundamental fact was "the creation of an inferior social and economic organization of exploiters and exploited." Sugar, tobacco, and cotton required the large plantation and hordes of cheap labor, and the small farm of the exindentured white servant could not possibly survive. The tobacco of the small farm in Barbados was displaced by the sugar of the large plantation. The rise of the sugar industry in the Caribbean was the signal for a gigantic dispossession of the small farmer. Barbados in 1645 had 11,200 small white farmers and 5,680 Negro slaves; in 1677 there were 745 large plantation owners and 82,023 slaves. In 1645 the island had 18,300 whites fit to bear arms, in 1667 only 8,300. . . .

Negro slavery therefore was only a solution, in certain historical circumstances, of the Caribbean labor problem. Sugar meant labor—at times that labor has been slave, at other times nominally free; at times black, at other times white or brown or yellow. Slavery in no way implied, in any scientific sense, the inferiority of the Negro. Without it the great development of the Caribbean sugar plantations, between 1650 and 1850, would have been impossible.

David Eltis

The Cultural Roots of African Slavery

Williams mentions in passing that Europeans did not enslave other Europeans. Canadian historian David Eltis, a specialist in Atlantic migration at Queens University, makes that issue the center of his analysis. He argues that Africans were not enslaved simply for economic reasons, for it would have been more convenient and probably cheaper to bring enslaved Europeans to the New World. He also suggests it was not prejudice against blacks that produced the African slave trade, but the unconscious exemption from enslavement Europeans gave themselves. Thus, Eltis endorses a cultural explanation for slavery.

David Eltis, "Cultural Roots of African Slavery," from *The Rise of African Slavery in the Americas*, 2000, pp. 64–72, 78–80, 83–84. Reprinted by permission of Cambridge University Press.

If we wish to understand the origins of African slavery in the New World or indeed in the pre-Columbian Old World, we must first explore the labor options of early modern Europeans—both those that were tried and those that were not. Second, we need to assess how close Europeans came to imposing slavery or slavelike conditions on other Europeans and finally what for them set slavery apart as a status for others. These steps will help clarify the cultural and ideological parameters that at once shaped the evolution of African New World slavery and kept Europeans as non-slaves. . . .

Although there is no evidence that Europeans ever considered instituting full chattel slavery of Europeans in their overseas settlements, the striking paradox is that no sound economic reasons spoke against it. By the seventeenth century, the most cursory examination of relative costs suggests that European slaves should have been preferred to either European indentured labor or African slaves. And while native Americans were cheap to enslave, their life expectancy and productivity in post-Columbian plantation conditions hardly compared with that of pre-industrial or, indeed, post-industrial Europeans. . . .

Moreover, . . . there were elements in the master-servant relationship in all European states in the late medieval period that could, and in several cases did, provide the basis for a revival of serfdom. And, if serfdom, why not slavery? Serfdom had disappeared in Sweden, Scotland, and the Low Countries no later than the early fourteenth century. But the institution not so much reappeared as appeared for the first time in Eastern Europe after these dates—and on a large scale. As already noted, marginal elements of European societies—convicts and vagrants—might have been candidates for forced labor in the Americas, but not only these. As late as the immediate antebellum period, there were ideologues in the southern United States who advocated slavery for poor whites as well as blacks.

From the strictly economic standpoint there were strong arguments in support of using European rather than African slave labor. The crux of the matter was shipping costs, which comprised by far the greater part of the price of imported bonded labor in the Americas. First, although the wind system of the Atlantic reduced the differential somewhat, it was normally quicker to sail directly to the Americas from Europe than to sail via Africa. In addition mortality and morbidity among both crews and passengers (or slaves) were lower in the north Atlantic than in the south. If we take into account the time spent collecting a slave cargo on the African coast as well, then the case for sailing directly from Europe with a cargo of Europeans appears stronger again. In the 1680s the Royal African Company (RAC) would often hire ships to carry slaves on its behalf. The hire rate was typically between £5 and £6 per slave landed alive in the Americas—a price that was understood to cover the full cost of sailing to Africa, acquiring slaves, and carrying them to the RAC's agents in the West Indies. The return cargo from the Americas was a separate speculation. The cost of shipping convicts to Barbados and the Leeward Islands at this time was similar. As noted later, however, ships carrying convicts, indentured servants, and fare-paying passengers always carried far fewer people per ton than did slave ships. There is little doubt that if ships carrying Europeans had been as closely packed as those carrying Africans, costs per person would have been much lower for Europeans than for Africans.

A further reason for using European rather than African slave labor derives from relative prices of African slaves and convict English labor—the nearest the English came to using Europeans as chattel slaves. Unskilled male convicts from England and Ireland sold for £16 each in Maryland in the years 1767–75 at a time when newly arrived African male slaves in the prime age group were selling for about triple this amount in Virginia and Maryland. The British males worked for ten years or less, the Africans for life. If convicts and their descendants had been sold into a lifetime of service, it is reasonable to suppose that planters would have been ready to pay a higher price for them. At this higher price, the British government and merchants might have found ways to provide more convicts. Shipping costs alone would not have interfered with the process. From this standpoint, convicts could have been sold into lifelong servitude for a price little more than that for seven or ten years of labor. Thus in the absence of an improbably rapid decline in slave prices as buyers switched from Africans to Europeans, we might suppose that there were no shipping cost barriers to European slaves forming the basis of the plantation labor forces of the Americas. . . .

Indeed enslavement in Europe might have been less costly than its African counterpart. First, transportation costs, which loomed so large within Africa, were bound to be lower in a subcontinent where major population centers were located near navigable waters. . . . Second, population growth in western Europe in general, and England in particular, was considerable during the era of the slave trade. Despite a net migration of 2.7 million from the mid-sixteenth to mid-nineteenth century, England's population rose sevenfold. Scholars debate the impact on the African population of the loss of twelve million people to the Americas. It is certain that this number of additional emigrants from a more heavily populated Europe over the same period would have had a negligible effect. Arguments that Africans could stand up to the epidemiology of the Caribbean are irrelevant here. Whatever the European-African mortality differentials, a hostile disease environment was never enough to prevent European indentured servants from working in the Caribbean sugar sector. Medical evidence would be pertinent only if Europeans had never labored in the Caribbean under any labor regime or if European slavery had been tried and found wanting because of excess mortality. In fact, peoples of Europe and Africa died prematurely for different reasons in the Caribbean, but life expectancies for the two groups were not very different. . . .

In fact, nearly one thousand convicts a year left Britain in the half-century after 1718. This may not seem like many compared to an African slave trade drawing twenty-five thousand a year from Africa in the last third of the seventeenth century and rising to an average of fifty thousand a year in the half century after 1700. Yet consider that the population of England was only 7 percent that of Europe in 1680, and, if the rest of Europe had followed the English practice in proportion, fourteen thousand convicts would have been available. A traffic in degredados from Portuguese possessions to Brazil and Angola existed from the sixteenth to the nineteenth century, and the massive fortifications at Havana and San Juan, as well as Spanish outposts in North Africa, were built in part with Iberian convicts. Germanic states that lacked maritime facilities sold convicts to Italian city states for galley service. In France about a thousand convicts a year arrived at Marseille in the later seventeenth and early eighteenth centuries, but these were all male and mostly between twenty and thirty-five years of age. The potential for a large, more demographically representative traffic in French convicts is clear.

Possible sources other than convicts were numerous. Prisoners from wars, as in Africa, could have provided many additional plantation laborers. The English were well aware of the cheap labor possibilities of the latter. Just when sugar production in Barbados was expanding most rapidly and within a year or two of their acquisition of Jamaica, the English used Scottish prisoners taken at the Battle of Dunbar and Dutch prisoners (taken from Dutch naval vessels) to help drain the fens. Indeed, when in rebellion, the Irish and Scots alone could have filled the labor needs of the English colonies. Nor does this speculation fully incorporate vagrants and the poor. A properly exploited system drawing on convicts, prisoners, and vagrants from all countries of Europe could easily have provided fifty thousand forced migrants a year without serious disruption to either international peace or existing social institutions that generated and supervised these potential European victims. If such an outflow had been directed to the plantation colonies, it is also unlikely that mercantilist statesmen would have questioned either the scale or the direction of the flow.

More specifically, British convicts could have replaced African slaves in the Chesapeake, the destination of most transport ships. The first recorded shipment of convicts dates to 1615. Until 1770 the number of convict arrivals was at least two-thirds that of slaves in total, although in the 1730s and 1740s slave arrivals were between two and four times larger. If all whites and their subsequent progeny sent against their will to the colonies had been accorded the slave status of African immigrants, there is no reason why the number of white slaves in Maryland and Virginia would not have been at least as large as the actual black slave population at the end of the colonial period. . . .

Given these transportation and production cost advantages European slave labor would have been no more expensive and probably substantially cheaper. Slavery in the Americas (white slavery) would have been extensive in the sixteenth and seventeenth centuries before African slaves arrived in large numbers. Plantations would have developed more quickly and European consumers would have enjoyed an accelerated flow of sugar and tobacco. The fact that African slavery in the Americas took longer to evolve than any European counterpart would have done—at least in North America—is accounted for by the greater costs of moving people from Africa as opposed to Europe.

It was, of course, inconceivable that any of the labor pools mentioned earlier (convicts, prisoners of war, or vagrants) could have been converted into chattel slaves. The barrier to European slaves in the Americas lay not only beyond shipping and enslavement costs but also beyond any strictly economic sphere. The English Vagrancy Act of 1547 prescribing slavery was never enforced. The seventy-two English political prisoners who were taken at Salisbury in 1654 and sent to Barbados the next year claimed to be "[f]ree-born People of this Nation, now in Slavery" and were able to petition Parliament in 1659; they occasioned an extensive discussion there not extended to Africans for another 130 years. There were serfs in Scotland as we have seen but there were no slaves. Across the English Channel a 1716 law was necessary to deny slaves brought privately to France their enfranchisement when they arrived in the country. In Spain, Portugal, and all Mediterranean countries by the sixteenth century, Moors and Africans could be slaves. Christians, which meant in practice Europeans, because non-Europeans who became Christian remained slaves, could not. Even Jews were less likely to be enslaved in Spain by the later Middle Ages. In 1492, they were expelled, not enslaved. . . .

Throughout Europe the state could take the lives of individuals in Europe, but enslavement was no longer an alternative to death; rather it had become a fate worse than death and as such was reserved for non-Europeans. Europeans would accept lawbreakers and prisoners as slaves only if they were not fellow Europeans. Conceptions of insider had expanded to include the European subcontinent whereas for Africans and American Indians a less than continent-wide definition of insider still pertained. In a profound but scarcely novel sense chattel slavery for Africans and Indians in the Americas was thus a function of the non-slave status that Europeans considered appropriate for themselves—a situation with historical parallels in many slave societies. . . .

States, merchants, and consumers of plantation produce all stood to gain from shipping convicts, prisoners, and indeed indentured servants in slavelike conditions. The fact that they did not do so says something about the views that European merchants and ultimately European societies held on the status of different migrant groups. Few societies in history have enslaved people they consider to be their own. . . . The relevant issue was who was to be considered "their own." In some African societies shared ethnicity and language might even mean an increased likelihood of enslavement—at least for women and children—given the focus on kin groups and their expansion through absorption of outsiders. In the Americas, slave raids of one Iroquois nation on another were not uncommon. But in western Europe, even the most degraded member of European society was spared enslavement. Only in the rather limited case of Amerindians in the Spanish Americas was such treatment extended to non-Europeans. This barrier was akin to the Muslim bar against the enslavement of non-Muslims, not in the sense that the basis of enslavement was religious, but rather that in both Muslim and Christian societies slavery came to be mainly African despite the fact that in both, slaves often converted to the faith of their owners. . . .

Explanations for these attitudes are more difficult to establish than the fact that such attitudes existed. . . . From one side of the ideological divide such reluctance might appear as a function of shared community values; from the other, it points to the resistance that would have inevitably followed or else manipulation on the part of the elite. The most serious strike in the preindustrial northeastern coal industry occurred in 1765 when mine owners attempted to follow their Scottish counterparts down a road that led to serfdom for workers. But what seems incontestable is that in regard to slavery the sense of the appropriate was shared across social divisions and cannot easily be explained by ideological differences or power relationships among classes. Outrage at the treatment of Africans was rarely expressed at any level of society before the late eighteenth century. The moral economy of the English crowd, like the various Christian churches, was preoccupied with other issues. When the immorality of coerced labor was recognised, the recognition appeared across all social groups at about the same time. Attempts to account for the failure of Europeans to enslave their own in terms of solidarity among the potential slaves do not seem promising. If the elite could kill Irish, Huguenots, Jews, prisoners of war, convicts, and many other marginalised groups, why could they not enslave them? The English considered those from the Celtic fringe different from themselves but, after the eleventh century at least, not different enough to enslave. For elite and non-elite alike enslavement remained a fate for which only non-Europeans were qualified.

David Brion Davis

Ideas and Institutions from the Old World

In summarizing a lifetime's study of slavery, retired Yale historian David Brion Davis considers the rise of New World slavery in a broader geographical and temporal perspective than Williams or Eltis, both of whom concentrate their attention on early modern English colonies. Davis suggests that haphazard developments in the medieval Islamic world reinforced

From David Brion Davis, *Inhuman Bondage: The Rise and Fall of Slavery in the New World*, 2006, pp. 78–85. Reprinted by permission of Oxford University Press.

European prejudices and that Europeans introduced African slavery and the sugar plantation system from the Mediterranean into the Atlantic and across to the Americas.

In the past, many historians, including Marxists, accepted a model of "economic determinism" when discussing the origins of New World slavery and the restriction of enslavement to Native Americans and then almost exclusively to sub-Saharan Africans and their descendants. Presenting racial slavery as an economically backward but inevitable and temporary stage in historical development, given the shortage of labor and the almost limitless expanses of land in the Americas, they tended to ignore or underestimate cultural and ideological factors, especially religion.

Yet there is now a broad consensus that plantation slavery, far from being archaic, was not only highly productive but anticipated much of the efficiency, organization, and global interconnectedness of industrial capitalism. The economic historian David Eltis has also argued that if only economic forces had prevailed, western Europeans would have revived white slavery, since it would have been much cheaper to enslave and transport white vagabonds, criminals, and prisoners of war to the New World than to sail all the way to West Africa and purchase increasingly expensive slaves in such a distant region. But the first option, Eltis stresses, was negated by whatever cultural forces had brought a sense of unity and freedom to Christians of western Europe, thus blocking the possibility of any significant revival of white slavery.

Turning to the influence of religions, the long struggles between Christianity and Islam and the cultures they generated have seldom been given sufficient attention with respect to the changing sources of slave labor. For well over a millennium, the ultimate division between "Us" and "Them," or "the Other," a paradigm for the polarity between masters and slaves, was nourished by the Muslim invasions of eastern and western Europe; by the Christian crusades into Muslim territories; by the Christian reconquest of Portugal, Spain, and the Mediterranean islands; and by the Muslim enslavement, from the 1500s to the early 1800s of well over a million western Europeans from Italy, France, Spain, Portugal, Holland, and Britain.

Some of these whites, who had been seized at sea or taken in large numbers along the European coasts from Italy to England and even Iceland, were ransomed by Europeans and publicly celebrated as symbols of the inherent freedom and "non-enslaveability" of Christian whites—a concept that began to develop in Byzantium in the early Middle Ages, when enslavement and ransoming first became linked with religious identity. In England especially, this ceremonial liberation of English captives—who often appeared in urban parades wearing their chains and tattered slave clothing—coincided in the eighteenth century with a growing desire to dignify "free labor," along with the king of new nationalism signified in the early eighteenth century by James Thompson's famous lines that would become a kind of national anthem: "Rule, Britannia! Britannia rules the waves . . . Britons never will be slaves.

As can be seen in their almost continuous wars, especially the ferocious Thirty Years' War from 1618 to 1648, western Europeans had few qualms about slaughtering and torturing one another, or even about exterminating civilians. Yet their own convicts, vagabonds, and prisoners of war were exempt from the kind of enslavement that seemed appropriate for Moors and then for what the English termed "Blackamoors."

I do not mean to minimize the importance of greed, economic self-interest, and an increasing desire for greater productivity and profit, all of which lay at the heart of early modern and modern slavery. But these economic desires were also fused with issues of identity, ideology, and power.

[There are] at least four cultural preconditions for the antiblack racism that dominated the white settlement and development of the Americas, especially from the late seventeenth century onward.

First . . . there were the strong sanctions for slavery in the West's religious and philosophical heritage extending back to the Hebrew and Christian Bibles and to the classical literature of the Greco-Roman era. Thus chattel slavery remained an acceptable institution even after it had disappeared from northwest Europe and after the Barbary corsairs underscored the belief that Christians from western Europe could not be legitimately enslaved.

Ironically, the revival and rediscovery of classical learning—supposedly a liberating step toward progress—gave new support for slavery in the Renaissance. But whereas Roman slaves had included virtually all the ethnic groups then available, the emerging modern world would be more influenced by the ancient Israelite distinction between Hebrew and enemy Canaanite slaves, and by the Islamic laws against forcibly enslaving free Muslims. This need to enslave "outsiders," except in Russia and parts of eastern Europe, which differed in demography and cultural traditions, also tied in with the ancient Greco-Roman conviction that external facial and physical traits correlated with internal mental and characterological strengths and weaknesses that were hereditary even if originally derived from climate and geography.

The second precondition . . . was the medieval Arab precedent of enslaving and transporting by ship or caravan enormous numbers of black Africans, who came to be seen as especially suited for the most degrading forms of work. In marked contrast to the enslaved Europeans in North Africa, hardly any of these black slaves were redeemed by their own people, though many were converted to Islam and some were freed by their owners.

Third, there is evidence suggesting that racist stereotypes as well as a racist interpretation of the biblical "Curse of Ham" were transmitted by Iberian Muslims to Christians, who by the 1400s were already becoming obsessed with the alleged danger that Jews and New Christians posed to their own "purity of blood." This incipient racism was then magnified in the fifteenth century when the Portuguese imported increasing numbers of West African slaves, who were auctioned in Lisbon or shipped to Spanish cities from Seville to Valencia. Still, unlike England, which deported its small Jewish population in 1290 and attempted to deport its small number of blacks in the late 1500s, Spain and Portugal absorbed much Jewish and especially Moorish culture. Despite Spain's expulsion of Jews and then Moriscos (converted Moors), Iberians became accustomed to the coexistence of a range of skin colors from black to white—a fact of life that would lead to a greater acceptance of racial intermixture in their future colonies in the New World.

This point, particularly when we take account of the much lighter-skinned people of northwestern Europe, brings us back to a fourth and final precondition: the negative connotations and symbolism of the "color" black . . . . [T]he deeply imprinted visual memories derived from depictions of black demons, devils, and torturers could and no doubt did reinforce other factors in creating a perception of the ultimate Outsiders, even more alien than Arabs and Jews, as the blacks from distant and pagan Africa. If some popes could welcome delegations of black Christians from Jerusalem and Ethiopia, Portugal's "discovery" of West Africa brought papal approval of black slavery and even the shipment of some black slaves as gifts to popes and their friends in Rome. . . .

In the beginning, however, the European maritime nations, from Spain and Portugal in the 1500s to France and England in the 1600s, did not undertake New World colonization with the intent of relying on African slaves (South Carolina is arguably an exception). Despite the importance of the preconditions we have considered, the New World of 1750 emerged from a long series of fortuitous, haphazard, and even catastrophic events, especially as the Mediterranean patterns of piracy, banditry, plunder, cruelty, and ruthless reprisals were transferred to the Caribbean. In Central America, for example, where the conquistadores were disappointed by the absence of tribute in comparison with Mexico, they found some compensation by branding Indian slaves on the face and shipping some sixty-seven thousand to Panama, Peru, and the Caribbean. In the sixteenth and seventeenth centuries the colonizing powers relied heavily on Indian labor, and in the seventeenth century the British in Barbados and Virginia depended for many decades on a large flow of white indentured servants, who long outnumbered black slaves.

Moving back again to origins, Venetian and Genoese merchants were at the forefront in developing conquered Arab sugar-producing regions in the Mediterranean, in supplying non-African slaves for a variety of economic needs in addition to sugar production, and finally in extending the system for slave-grown sugar to the so-called Atlantic islands of Madeira, the Canaries, the Cape Verdes, and São Tomé, off the west coast of Africa. Here, in order to grasp a more global picture, we should mention again the changing sources of slave labor from the 1200s to the late 1400s, a subject that highlights shifting boundaries and provides perspective on the ultimate choice of Africans.

Following the Western capture of Constantinople, in the Fourth Crusade (1204), Italian merchants participated in a booming long-distance seaborne trade that transported tens of thousands of "white" Armenian, Bulgarian, Circassian, Mingrelian, and Georgian slaves from regions around the Black Sea and the Sea of Azov to Mediterranean markets extending from Muslim Egypt and Syria to Christian Crete, Cyprus, Sicily, and eastern Spain. The slaves were used for the production of sugar as well as for numerous other services. What needs to be stressed is that the Tatars and other slave traders north of the Black Sea were as eager as their later African counterparts to march streams of captives, in this case mostly "white" captives, to shoreline markets where they could be exchanged for coveted goods.

Between 1414 and 1423 no fewer than ten thousand bondsmen (mostly bondswomen, to meet the demand for household servants) were sold in Florence alone. In the early 1400s this white slave trade from the Black Sea foreshadowed almost every aspect of the African slave trade, which was about to begin, including complex organization, permanent posts or forts for trade, and long-distance shipment by sea to multinational markets. In fact, although the Portuguese began importing black African slaves in the 1440s, the region between the Black and Caspian seas might conceivably have been a significant source of slaves for New World settlements after 1492 (and we have noted that a very few white "Eastern" slaves were shipped to Hispanic America).

But in 1453 the Ottoman Turks captured Constantinople and thus the entrance from the Mediterranean into the Black Sea. The Turks soon diverted the flow of Black Sea and Balkan captives solely to Islamic markets. Turkish expansion brought an end to Italian colonization efforts in the eastern Mediterranean and sharply reduced Europe's supply of sugar. The Turks also cut off Christian Europe from its major source of slaves, and for most potential buyers the price of slaves became prohibitive. Aside from captured Muslims, the only alternative to the Crimea and the steppes of western Asia (given the understood prohibition against enslaving western Europeans) was sub-Saharan Africa. For a time, this new demand stimulated the Arab caravan trade across the Sahara. Hence a very few black slaves taken to the shores of Libya and Tunisia were dispersed to Sicily, Naples, Majorca, southern France, and Mediterranean Spain. (In Sicily a notary recording in Latin referred to *sclavi negri*, literally "black Slavs," who outnumbered white slaves by the 1490s.)

At the same time, Genoese capital and technology had strengthened Portuguese sea power, and Portugal's harbors had proved to be ideal for the small ships, mostly owned by Italian merchants, that carried commodities from the Near East to England and western Europe. Some of the same Italian merchant and banking families long involved in the Black Sea slave trade now sent agents to Seville and Lisbon, where they became pioneers in developing the African slave trade. For example, Bartolomeo Marchionni, who represented one such family, moved in 1470 from Florence to Lisbon. He soon owned sugar plantations in Madeira, worked by black slaves, and the king of Portugal granted him a monopoly for slave trading on the Guinea coast. There could hardly be a clearer example of the continuity between the late medieval Black Sea—Mediterranean slave networks and the emerging Atlantic Slave System, both energized by the expansion and westward movement of sugar cultivation.

The Portuguese naval expedition to West Africa in the mid-1400s were originally intended to find wheat and barley, to outflank the Arab caravan trade, to find the rich sources of gold and pepper south of Mali, and perhaps to find "Prester John," a legendary Christian ruler somewhere beyond the Islamic world. In the event, Prince Henry's voyagers also initiated a direct slave trade between West Africa and Lisbon and began to colonize the uninhabited Madeira Islands, at first using as slaves the light-skinned Gaunche natives of the Canary Islands, who had also been enslaved and massacred by the Spaniards.

By the time of Columbus's first American voyage, in 1492, Madeira had already become a wealthy sugar colony mainly dependent on the labor of black African slaves. The Atlantic islands had originally been bases for pirates and sources for water and supplies for mariners; partly because they presented less risk of tropical diseases than the African mainland, they then became major sites of agricultural production. As the first true colony committed to sugar monoculture and increasingly to black slave labor, Madeira was the transitional prototype for later mercantilist ideals of empire. Madeira soon outstripped the entire Mediterranean in the production of sugar, which was reexported by the late 1490s to England, France, Italy, and even the eastern Mediterranean. Columbus, who had lived for over ten years on an island near Madeira, had the foresight to take sugarcane from the Spanish Canary Islands on his second voyage to the "Indies" in 1493.

Meanwhile, as early as 1495, São Tomé, situated much farther south, in the Gulf of Guinea, was shipping slave-grown sugar directly to Antwerp, long the major refining and distributing center for Europe. For the next half-century São Tomé would import more African slaves than Europe, the Americas, or the other Atlantic islands combined. Some wealthy Africans in Angola actually invested in sugar plantations on São Tomé, which also became a gathering place for slaves whom the Portuguese then sold to Africans in exchange for gold, or later shipped westward to the Americas. By 1507 there were about two thousand slaves working on São Tomé's sugar plantations and another five to six thousand awaiting reexport.

In summary, then, while African slaves were not part of original European blueprints for colonizing the Americas (except for South Carolina), spatial boundaries had shifted even by the 1490s in a way that would easily enable Europeans to draw on an enormous potential supply of African slave labor—aided, I should add, by the favorable system of Atlantic winds and currents, and by the later cultivation in Africa of such highly nutritious New World crops as manioc (or cassava), corn (maize), and squash, which had the long-term effect of greatly increasing the West African population.

Linda M. Heywood and John K. Thornton

European and African Cultural Differences

In contrast to the grand counterfactual argument of David Eltis, Boston University historians Linda M. Heywood and John K. Thornton emphasize the variety of ideas about the institution of slavery in North America in the 1600s. They combine their own extensive work on West Central Africans with terminology introduced by historian Ira Berlin, who distinguished the position of the Charter Generation (the first to arrive from Africa) from the more creolized Plantation Generation that followed. Berlin also introduced the term *Atlantic Creole* to describe Africans all around the Atlantic who had adopted many aspects of European culture, including language, naming, and religion. Heywood and Thornton echo the classic argument of the late Winthrop Jordan that English ideas of slavery were still evolving in early colonies and suggest that some of the puzzling diversity of opinion reflects the fact that Englishmen in this period regarded Christian Africans as more like themselves than they did uncreolized Africans.

Recent scholarship has . . . , identif[ied] racial slavery as a cultural as well as an economic system as unique in the Atlantic world, largely reacting toward the predominant paradigm that saw African slavery in New World societies and racism as being economically determined by the rise of capitalism.

From Linda M. Heywood and John K. Thornton, *Central Africans, Atlantic Creoles, and the Foundation of the Americas, 1585–1660,* 2007, pp. 294–296, 298–299, 312, 319–321, 327–331. Reprinted by permission of Cambridge University Press.

In 1997, Robin Blackburn, for example, in a comprehensive study of slavery in the various European colonies in the Americas, argued that Europeans found it easier to subject Africans to slavery, an institution that had greatly declined in their own societies in Europe, than to subject Europeans to it. Blackburn believed that the interpretations of the Biblical Curse of Ham found Africans to be degraded and thus suitable to be enslaved. In the same year James Sweet, addressing specifically slavery in the Iberian world, also pointed to hostile attitudes toward dark-skinned people derived from the heritage of the war against the Muslims and Christian teachings about the curse of Ham to explain racism and racial slavery in the Spanish and Portuguese Americas. David Eltis produced a systematic, economically driven analysis in 2000, arguing counterfactually that . . . it would have been both cost-effective and legal to use Europeans (convicts, vagabonds, and prisoners of war) as slaves in the Americas. However, Europeans did not take this option, he contended, because they considered the institution to be too harsh for cultural insiders, but they were willing to impose it on Africans, who they considered to be outsiders. Cultural studies and postcolonial literature have also contributed to the discussion by locating an ever wider range of ways—physical appearance, susceptibility to disease, skill, technology, and social and cultural norms—by which early modern Europeans distanced themselves from other peoples of the world.

This recent set of Atlantic focused studies actually revised and modified the work of Winthrop Jordan, whose landmark 1969 book, *White over Black*, on the origins of slavery in colonial North America (but actually the Chesapeake region) identified preexisting European racism as the primary cause of the institution. In the historiography of North America as in the discussion of slavery in general, however, Jordan's position was largely counterbalanced in the 1980s and 1990s by economic-driven arguments presented by Edmund Morgan, Russell Menard, and David Galenson (among others) that linked the origin of slavery in North America to the relative cost of indentured European and enslaved African labor or to issues of productivity.

The historical dilemma that engendered this debate concerned two central issues. the status of labor in the early settlement period in English North America (especially the Chesapeake), from roughly 1607 to 1676, and the role of racial prejudice in emergence of slavery. During this period, most workers were indentured servants of European origin, who served for limited periods and enjoyed some legal rights, giving way by the end of the period to an enslaved African labor force with very few rights. The legal conditions of the African who came during the early period seemed to the historians to resemble those of indentured servants more than slaves, and indeed some even argued that the Africans were simply regarded as indentured servants who were enslaved only later. For historians such as T. H. Breen and Stephen Innes or Douglas Deal, in the early period Africans were relatively well treated, shared space with European workers, and were frequently manumitted, and then could participate in the life of the community by bearing arms, appearing in court, and owing land. Because of the apparent ease of interaction and ability to improve one's status, many scholars saw this period as one of the challenged the idea that Africans were from the beginning held as slaves and accorded a degraded position. . . .

Ira Berlin's contention that the first Africans were Atlantic Creoles, which he advanced in 1997, changed the nature of the debate, as he argued that whatever notions Europeans might have had about Africans in general, those whom the Dutch and English brought to the early colonies appeared much more like insiders and some were treated as such. This attitude had an important impact on the institution of slavery, for he argued that the early period represented a society with slaves, rather than a slave society, and thus with greater access to freedom and rights. This, however, was not the case with the Africans who would follow them in the Plantation Generation. The relative insider status of the Charter Generation allowed members to negotiate pathways to freedom and relative political and legal equality in colonial North America.

Although we disagree with Ira Berlin on some of the specifics of his argument, we believe that his ideas concerning the relative ease of social mobility of the Charter Generation are correct. In [this essay] we address the contention that Europeans held uniformly negative attitudes about Africans and that this would contribute to their treatment by examining some of the most relevant of English and Dutch writings on Africa between 1450 and 1660. We show that they displayed a broad range of views, both positive and negative, which runs counter to the idea that European writing represented Africans in an entirely negative way and, moreover, that with regard to Central Africa, where most of the Charter Generation originated, their writings portray the people (especially in Kongo) very sympathetically. The following section contends that although the English and Dutch colonists did regard the first Africans as slaves and not as indentured servants, they had not yet defined slavery as lifelong, inheritable servitude but only as indefinitive service, which might explain their opportunities for expanded rights, including freedom, social acceptance, and mobility. Finally, we suggest that the Christian background of many Atlantic Creoles may have been the key that made these opportunities more attainable . . . .

In our view, both the English and Dutch regarded the majority of the first Africans they brought to their colonies as slaves, not as indentured servants, though a few did come as servants from Europe or the Caribbean. However, neither people defined slavery in the way that would become the norm for African forced labor after the mid-seventeenth century. The definition of slavery as lifetime, heritable servitude would develop only with the Plantation Generation. . . .

Although the English were aware of Portuguese and Spanish practice of slavery and the legal condition of slaves in their lands, they did not necessarily see slavery exactly as the Spanish and Portuguese did. They might view it as a long (perhaps even life-long) contract as seen in the act of the Barbados Assembly passed in 1636 that declared "negroes and Indians that came here to be sold, should serve for life unless a contract was before made to the contrary." Lord Mandeville, a member of the Somers Island Company that controlled Bermuda, wrote to Thomas Durham, "For the negroes I see no reason why they should deserve freedom from their service," clearly seeing their term as indeterminate and possibly indefinite. In fact, Robert McColley has argued that in the seventeenth century, *servant* meant both "slave" and "indentured servant." Indentured servants could be sold, exchanged, or passed on from one owner to another, and sometimes they, too, were acquired through capture. In 1640, Barbados received some kidnapped Frenchmen who were sold for 900 pounds of cotton a head. However, they had definite terms of service and in theory would be freed.

The idea that slavery was a permanent condition restricted to Africans was not firmly established in the English legal mind either, in spite of the Portuguese model. When Captain Jackson brought about a dozen Africans to Bermuda in 1637–1638, he sold them all to Hugh Wentworth with the stipulation that they serve 99-year indentures, certainly lifelong but not heritable. That same year, a certain Maria was sold to serve for 19 years. When Jackson returned to Bermuda in 1644 after a year-long privateering raid in the Spanish territories, he stipulated that another group of Africans he had taken were to serve shorter terms, some for 4, others of only 7 years. In his will of 1650, a Barbados man wished that "as for my negro he shall serve 21 years after the date hereof. And then to be free."

The fact that some Africans did come to the colonies as indentured servants has confused the issue of slavery as well. . . . But these Africans were exceptions, and the bulk of those people labeled negroes were probably regarded, as the Portuguese usage implied, as slaves.

But in English, the word *slave* did not have a fixed legal meaning of life-long, inheritable servitude in early-seventeenth-century America. English colonists often used the term *slave* as meaning "totally dependent," as when Francis Newman petitioned in 1620 that although he was "sent a freeman" to Virginia, he was "sustayinge great bondage and slavery" at the hands of Captain Argoll. Lewis Hughes of Bermuda similarly complained in 1621 that he will not be "merchant's slaves" with regard to the extension of credit. Elsewhere, Bermuda settlers complained in 1622 that "children [were] dying like slaves." . . .

Atlantic Creoles seem to have attained freedom remarkably easily, considering the later history of American servitude. This issue, the frequency with which they were manumitted, has been a key topic in the debate about the status of the Charter Generation. In 1972 Edmund Morgan, after examining the 1668 titheable list for Northampton County, Virginia, supported this idea when he reported that 29 percent of the Africans in that county were free, a figure that far exceeded the percentage of free African Americans at any subsequent point in American history.

Most of the discussion on the status of the first Africans in the English and Dutch colonies has centered on English and Dutch law and racial attitude. What the above discussion has revealed, however, is that the question is much more complex. A significant percentage of the first Africans were Atlantic Creoles and their ability to demonstrate that they were Christians facilitated their transition from slavery to freedom. Thus the best explanation that accounts for the large percentage of free people among the Charter Generation in the Dutch and English settlements may be more related to this fact than to loopholes in the law or the development of slavery. In contrast to the assumptions that the arriving Christians were converted in America, Ira Berlin identified the Creoles familiarity with European culture, including religion, and Graham Hodges specifically notes the connection between the Christian background of the Angolans coming to New Netherland and the high percentage who obtained manumission.

Both English and Dutch popular wisdom, if not law, maintained that a Christian could not hold another Christian as a slave. . . . Many Anglicans also believed that Christian Africans could not be held as slaves. In 1648, when the non-Christian West African Sambo expressed his desire to become a Christian, Richard Ligon, who was visiting Barbados at the time, intervened with Sambo's master on his behalf, but his master reminded his fellow Englishman that English law made it so that "we could not make a Christian a slave" and to make a slave a Christian would be to threaten the whole institution of slavery. If Ligon never met any Christian slaves during his stay in Barbados, Father Antoine Biet, a visiting French priest, met them. He reported that during his stay in Barbados those Africans who had "the Catholic religion which they have received amongst the Portuguese . . . keep it as best as they can, saying their prayers and worshiping God in their hearts." At about the same period the French priest Jean-Baptiste du Tertre reported that the English and Dutch would not convert their slaves to Christianity as they would no longer be slaves. These ideas still prevailed as late as the 1680s, when James II made a resolution that "the negroes upon the plantations should all be baptized, declaiming against that impiety of their masters prohibiting it since they believed that they would be ipso facto free." . . .

Africans who were Christians when they arrived were able to take advantage of the belief that Christians could not be held in slavery. In the English colonies, their names provide some indication of their Christian status. A clear case of this comes from the two early Jamestown censuses in which some Africans are listed with Iberian Christian names or English versions of them and others are listed just as "Negroes." A remarkable number of the manumitted Africans on the Eastern Shore bore Christian names. That "Antonio and Isabell" on the 1625 census are revealed to have "their child baptized" without further comment, it suggests that their Christian background was not questioned.

Records of Dutch manumissions in New Netherland reveal a similar pattern for the freed Africans. The names show that the Africans clearly brought the Iberian names with them, were self-identified and must have received the names through being raised in a Christian community (Kongo, Portuguese Angola, and the pockets of Christian communities as far east as Matamba) and not just through the nominal baptism in Luanda. . . .

The hardening of the laws in the 1660s explicitly excluded African Christians from using their religion to obtain manumission and also closed the avenue for freedom by excluding converts from using Christianity as a means to gain freedom. In Virginia and New Netherland they did so in the environment of the arrival of large numbers of West Africans, whose culture was different and more alien to Euro-American expectations. This influx of West Africans came with economic changes that eventually would affect law and close the door even for Central Africans, including the descendants of the manumitted Charter Generation.

PART

The Slave Trade Within Africa

VARIETY OF OPINION

[A] great body of the Negro inhabitants of Africa have continued [in a state of slavery] from the most early period of their history. . . . There are regular markets, where slaves . . . are bought and sold.

MUNGO PARK

Few of the [179] informants had spent much time as slaves. . . . [T]hey were enslaved in their home district and immediately taken down to the coast.

P. E. H. HAIR

Of 100 people seized in Africa, 75 would have reached the market-places in the interior; . . . 64 . . . would have arrived at the coast; . . . 57 would have boarded the ships; . . . and 48 or 49 would have lived to behold their first master in the New World.

JOSEPH C. MILLER

27

The strong preference of the slave sellers for guns . . . reinforces the slave-gun cycle theory according to which . . . slave gatherers bought more firearms to capture more slaves to buy more firearms.

JOSEPH E. INIKORI

[T]he more we know about African warfare and resulting enslavement, the less clear and direct the connections between war and the export of slaves becomes.

JOHN THORNTON

Mungo Park

West Africa in the 1790s

Until the last decades of the Atlantic trade there is very little direct evidence of the mechanisms that delivered slaves to Europeans at the coast. The Scotsman Mungo Park was one of the first Europeans to travel into inland regions of Africa and to observe how people became slaves. He found that most were prisoners taken in warfare and raids, but that others lost their free status as the result of famine, debt, or crimes. Captives were either kept as slaves in Africa or sold abroad.

The slaves in Africa, I suppose, are nearly in the proportion of three to one to the freemen. They claim no reward for their services, except food and cloathing; and are treated with kindness or severity, according to the good or bad disposition of their masters. Custom, however, has established certain rules with regard to the treatment of slaves, which it is thought dishonourable to violate. Thus, the domestic slaves, or such as are born in a man's own house, are treated with more lenity than those which are purchased with money. The authority of the master over the

From Mungo Park, *Travels in the Interior Districts of Africa: Performed in the Years 1795, 1796, and 1797* (London: John Murray, 1816).

domestic slave, as I have elsewhere observed, extends only to reasonable correction: for the master cannot sell his domestic, without having first brought him to a public trial, before the chief men of the place. But these restrictions on the power of the master extend not to the case of prisoners taken in war, nor to that of slaves purchased with money. All these unfortunate beings are considered as strangers and foreigners, who have no right to the protection of the law, and may be treated with severity, or sold to a stranger, according to the pleasure of their owners. There are, indeed, regular markets, where slaves of this description are bought and sold; and the value of a slave in the eye of an African purchaser, increases in proportion to his distance from his native kingdom; for when slaves are only a few days' journey from the place of their nativity, they frequently effect their escape: but when one or more kingdoms intervene, escape being more difficult, they are more readily reconciled to their situation. On this account, the unhappy slave is frequently transferred from one dealer to another, until he has lost all hopes of returning to his native kingdom. The slaves which are purchased by the Europeans on the Coast, are chiefly of this description; a few of them are collected in the petty wars, hereafter to be described, which take place near the Coast; but by far the greater number are brought down in large caravans from the inland countries, of which many are unknown, even by name, to the Europeans. The slaves which are thus brought from the interior, may be divided into two distinct classes: *first*, such as were slaves from their birth, having been born of enslaved mothers; *secondly*, such as were born free, but who afterwards, by whatever means, became slaves. Those of the first description are by far the most numerous; for prisoners taken in war (at least such as are taken in open and declared war, when one kingdom avows hostilities against another) are generally of this description. The comparatively small proportion of free people, to the enslaved, throughout Africa, has already been noticed; and it must be observed, that men of free condition, have many advantages over the slaves, even in war time. They are in general better armed, and well mounted; and can either fight or escape with some hopes of success, but the slaves, who have only their spears and bows, and of whom great numbers are loaded with baggage, become an easy prey. Thus, when Mansong, King of Bambarra, made war upon Kaarta . . . , he took in one day nine hundred prisoners, of which number not more than seventy were free men. This account I received from Daman Jumma, who had thirty slaves at Kemmoo, all of whom were made prisoners by Mansong. Again, when a freeman is taken prisoner, his friends will sometimes ransom him by giving two slaves in exchange; but when a slave is taken, he has no hopes of such redemption. . . .

Slaves of the second description, generally become such by one or other of the following causes, 1. *Captivity.* 2. *Famine.* 3. *Insolvency.* 4. *Crimes.* A freeman may, by the established customs of Africa, become a slave by being taken in war. War is, of all others, the most productive source, and was probably the origin of slavery; for when one nation had taken from another, a greater number of captives than could be exchanged on equal terms, it is natural to suppose that the conquerors, finding it inconvenient to maintain their prisoners, would compel them to labour; at first, perhaps, only for their own support; but afterwards to support their masters. Be this as it may, it is a known fact, that prisoners of war in Africa, are the slaves of the conquerors; and when the weak or unsuccessful warrior, begs for mercy beneath the uplifted spear of his opponent, he gives up at the same time his claim to liberty; and purchases his life at the expence of his freedom. . . .

The wars of Africa are of two kinds, which are distinguished by different appellations: that species which bears the greatest resemblance to our European contests, is denominated *killi*, a word signifying "to call out," because such wars are openly avowed, and previously declared. Wars of this description in Africa, commonly terminate, however, in the course of a single campaign. A battle is fought, the vanquished seldom think of rallying again; the whole inhabitants become panic struck; and the conquerors have only to bind the slaves, and carry off their plunder and their victims. Such of the prisoners as, through age or infirmity, are unable to endure fatigue, or are found unfit for sale, are considered as useless; and I have no doubt are frequently put to death. The same fate commonly awaits a chief, or any other person who has taken a very distinguished part in the war. And here it may be observed that, notwithstanding this exterminating system, it is surprising to behold how soon an African town is rebuilt and repeopled. The circumstance arises probably from this; that their pitched battles are few; the weakest know their own situation, and seek safety in flight. When their country has been desolated, and their ruined towns and villages deserted by the enemy, such of the inhabitants as have escaped the *sword*, and the *chain*, generally return, though with cautious steps, to the place of their nativity; for it seems to be the universal wish of mankind, to spend the evening of their days where they passed their infancy. . . .

The other species of African warfare is distinguished by the appellation of *tegria*, "plundering or stealing." It arises from a sort of hereditary feud which the inhabitants of one nation or district bear towards another. No immediate cause of hostility is assigned, or notice of attack given; but the inhabitants of each watch every opportunity to plunder and distress the objects of their animosity by predatory excursions. These are very common, particularly about the beginning of the dry season, when the labour of the harvest is over and provisions are plentiful. Schemes of vengeance are then meditated. The chief man surveys the number and activity of his vassals, as they brandish their spears at festivals; and elated with his own importance, turns his whole thoughts towards revenging some depredation or insult, which either he or his ancestors may have received from a neighbouring state.

Wars of this description are generally conducted with great secrecy. A few resolute individuals, headed by some person of enterprise and courage, march quietly through the woods, surprise in the night some unprotected village, and carry off the inhabitants and their effects, before their neighbours can come to their assistance. One morning, during my stay at Kamalia, we were all much alarmed by a party of this kind. The king of Fooladoo's son, with five hundred horsemen, passed secretly through the woods, a little to the southward of Kamalia, and on the morning following plundered three towns belonging to Madigai, a powerful chief in Jallonkadoo.

The success of this expedition encouraged the governor of Bangassi, a town of Fooladoo, to make a second inroad upon another part of the same country. Having assembled about two hundred of his people, he passed the river Kokoro in the night, and carried off a great number of prisoners. Several of the inhabitants who had escaped these attacks, were afterwards seized by the Mandingoes, as they wandered about in the woods or concealed themselves in the glens and strong places of the mountains.

These plundering excursions always produce speedy retaliation; and when large parties cannot be collected for this purpose, a few friends will combine together, and advance into the enemy's country, with a view to plunder, or carry off the inhabitants. A single individual has been known to take his bow and quiver, and proceed in like manner. Such an attempt is doubtless in him an act of rashness; but when it is considered that in one of these predatory wars, he has probably been deprived of his child, or his nearest relation, his situation will rather call for pity than censure. The poor sufferer, urged on by the feelings of domestic or paternal attachment, and the ardour of revenge, conceals himself among the bushes, until some young or unarmed person passes by. He then, tiger-like, springs upon his prey; drags his victim into the thicket, and in the night carries him off as a slave.

When a Negro has, by means like these, once fallen into the hands of his enemies, he is either retained as the slave of his conqueror, or bartered into a distant kingdom; for an African, when he has once subdued his enemy, will seldom give him an opportunity of lifting up his hand against him at a future period. A conqueror commonly disposes of his captives according to the rank which they held in their native kingdom. Such of the domestic slaves as appear to be of a mild disposition, and particularly the young women, are retained as his own slaves. Others that display marks of discontent, are disposed of in a distant country; and such of the freemen or slaves, as have taken an active part in the war, are either sold to the Slatees, or put to death. War, therefore, is certainly the most general, and most productive source of slavery; and the desolations of war often (but not always) produce the second cause of slavery, *famine*; in which case a freeman becomes a slave to avoid a greater calamity.

Perhaps, by a philosophic and reflecting mind, death itself would scarcely be considered as a greater calamity than slavery; but the poor Negro, when fainting with hunger, thinks like Esau of old; *"behold I am at the point to die, and what profit shall this birthright do to me?"* There are many instances of free men voluntarily surrendering up their liberty to save their lives. During a great scarcity which lasted for three years, in the countries of the Gambia, great numbers of people became slaves in this manner. . . . Large families are very often exposed to absolute want: and as the parents have almost unlimited authority over their children, it frequently happens, in all parts of Africa, that some of the latter are sold to purchase provisions for the rest of the family. When I was at Jarra, Daman Jumma pointed out to me three young slaves which he had purchased in this manner. I have already related another instance which I saw at Wonda: and I was informed that in Fooladoo, at that time, it was a very common practice.

The third cause of slavery, is *insolvency*. Of all the offences (if insolvency may be so called) to which the laws of Africa have affixed the punishment of slavery, this is the most common. A Negro trader commonly contracts debts on some mercantile speculation, either from his neighbours, to purchase such articles as will sell to advantage in a distant market, or from the European traders on the Coast; payment to be made in a given time. In both cases, the situation of the adventurer is exactly the same. If he succeeds, he may secure an independency. If he is unsuccessful, his person and services are at the disposal of another; for, in Africa, not only the effects of the insolvent, but even the insolvent himself, are sold to satisfy the lawful demands of his creditors.

The fourth cause above enumerated, is *the commission of crimes, on which the laws of the country affix slavery as a punishment.* In Africa, the only offences of this class are murder, adultery, and witchcraft; and I am happy to say, that they did not appear to me to be common. In cases of murder, I was informed, that the nearest relation of the deceased had it in his power, after conviction, either to kill the offender with his own hand, or sell him into slavery. When adultery occurs, it is generally left to the option of the person injured, either to sell the culprit, or accept such a ransom for him as he may think equivalent to the injury he has sustained. By witchcraft, is meant pretended magic, by which the lives or healths of persons are affected: in other words, it is the administering of poison. No trial for this offence, however, came under my observation while I was in Africa; and I therefore suppose that the crime, and its punishment, occur but very seldom.

When a freeman has become a slave by any one of the causes before mentioned, he generally continues so for life, and his children (if they are born of an enslaved mother) are brought up in the same state of servitude. There are, however, a few instances of slaves obtaining their freedom, and sometimes even with the consent of their masters; as by performing some singular piece of service, or by going to battle, and bringing home two slaves as a ransom; but the common way of regaining freedom is by escape; and when slaves have once set their minds on running away, they often succeed. Some of them will wait for years before an opportunity presents itself, and during that period shew no signs of discontent. In general, it may be remarked that slaves who come from a hilly country, and have been much accustomed to hunting and travel, are more apt to attempt their escape, than such as are born in a flat country, and have been employed in cultivating the land.

Such are the general outlines of that system of slavery which prevails in Africa; and it is evident from its nature and extent, that it is a system of no modern date. It probably had its origin in the remote ages of antiquity, before the Mahomedans explored a path across the Desert. How far it is maintained and supported by the slave traffic, which, for two hundred years, the nations of Europe have carried on with the natives of the Coast, it is neither within my province, nor in my power, to explain. If my sentiments should be required concerning the effect which a discontinuance of that commerce would produce on the manners of the natives, I should have no hesitation in observing, that, in the present unenlightened state of their minds, my opinion is, the effect would neither be so extensive or beneficial, as many wise and worthy persons fondly expect.

P. E. H. Hair

African Narratives of Enslavement

In this selection, Professor Paul Hair (1926–2001) analyzes the many tales of enslavement collected by a German missionary in Sierra Leone from Africans rescued from slave ships by British patrols in the first part of the nineteenth century. He enhances the value of these rare accounts by actual slaves by identifying where they came from and grouping them by the causes of their enslavement. His results are very close to Park's impressions, except for a much lower incidence of people born into slavery.

S. W. Koelle in his *Polyglotta Africana* of 1854 . . . supplied notes on 210 informants, but only 179 were definitely stated to be ex-slaves. . . . Of the ex-slaves, 177 were men and 2 women. Koelle chose these informants, out of the 40,000 or so ex-slaves in the Freetown district in 1850, because each individual (occasionally, two individuals) represented a different African language. Hence . . . the informants were drawn from a very large number of language groups, covering a large part of West and West Central Africa and a few outlying districts in East Africa.

P. E. H. Hair, "African Narratives of Enslavement" from "The Enslavement of Koelle's Informants," *Journal of African History*, 6.2, 1965, pp. 193–201. Reprinted by permission of Cambridge University Press.

Though the societies involved were so various and so scattered, the accounts of the informants' enslavement, analysed below, suggest a general pattern of reaction to the economic and social opportunities—and intrusions—of the slave trade. . . . [Because] we have available here only 179 biographical records of a process involving many millions of unrecorded life-histories . . . , we take care to indicate the provenance—by language—of each informant discussed in any detail. (The first name given is always Koelle's name for the language: while the name in capitals is either the modern name for the language, or the name of a better known grouping which includes the language. . . .)

. . . [A]lmost all were enslaved before they were forty; three-quarters were enslaved before they were thirty; one-half were enslaved during their twenties. . . . The earliest enslavement date was 1795, the latest 1847. Three-quarters of the informants had been enslaved—that is, in almost all cases, had left their homeland—more than ten years before the date of interview; and nearly half had been enslaved more than twenty years before. The oldest man interviewed was probably nearly eighty, the youngest was in his early twenties. . . .

Few of the informants had spent much time as slaves. Five of them had spent periods of years in America (and had come to Freetown after emancipation), and twenty nine had spent periods of years in Africa, mainly as slaves to Africans. The remainder had reached Sierra Leone shortly after enslavement (though an exact period of months or years was seldom stated); that is, they were enslaved in their home district and immediately taken down to the coast (a journey which occasionally took many months, however), and were shortly afterwards captured aboard a slave ship and brought straightway to Freetown. . . .

Manner of Enslavement: (a) War

Forty-eight of the informants (34% of those detailing their manner of enslavement) had been "taken in war." Twenty-five of these, and two who had been "kidnapped," were taken by the Fula during their razzias. These extended from the Futa Jalon (modern Guinea) to Adamawa (Cameroons). Thus, two Soso/SUSU were captured by the Fula c. 1820 and c. 1830, while about a dozen men from tribes of Adamawa and the North Cameroons provided evidence of Fula raids from 1820 onwards.

About his twenty-fourth year [c. 1825], a people came from a far and unknown country, who were called Beliyi or Bedeyi, and burnt all their towns, the capital not excepted, so that all who could run, escaped into the woods. There he [an Afudu/TANGALE] was caught by them. . . .

Two years before Nyamsi, or Andrew Wilhelm of Freetown, [a Param/ BAMILEKE] was kidnapped [c. 1825], the Tebale had invaded his country and committed the most ferocious atrocities: e.g., they took children by their legs and dashed their brains out against trees: ripped up the pregnant women: caught four hundred children of the King's family and the families of other great men, made a large fire, and burnt them alive. . . .

Here he may also be mentioned the JAR man who, as a boy of twelve was sent to the Fula emir of Bauchi, as part of the annual tribute of slaves. But the Fula biter was sometimes bit:

Adamu, or Edward Klein of Freetown [a Fulbe/FULA] brought up in Kano, had been five years married to his two wives when he had to join the annual war-expedition [in 1845] against the Maladis, an independent Hausa tribe, on which occasion they had to flee from the Maladis and he was caught in the flight by night. This enabled the Maladis who had caught him to carry him to another country by stealth, and to sell him there: for there is a law among the Maladis that all Fulbe taken in war are to be killed forthwith.

Manner of Enslavement: (b) Kidnapping

Forty-three of Koelle's informants (30%) stated that they had been "kidnapped" into slavery. Many gave no further details and appear to have been kidnapped by fellow-tribesmen. . . . Travel outside the homelands was dangerous.

Sem, or Peter Kondo of Gloucester, [a Kaure/TEM] born in the village Wuram, where he was brought up and was probably upwards of thirty years old when he was kidnapped in the Basare country, where he had gone to buy corn.

Yapanda, or William Seck of Wellington, [a Tiwi/TIV], born in the village of Torowo, where he lived till his twenty-fourth year, when he was kidnapped on a trading-tour to Hausa.

William Harding, an Ondo/YORUBA, was kidnapped on a trading journey by the Ijesha/YORUBA. An Abaja/IBO and an Oworo/YORUBA were each kidnapped by "a treacherous friend." The treacherous friend of a Muntu/YAO enticed him on board a Portuguese ship and then took money for him. A Bagbalang/GRUSI was kidnapped at the instigation of his brother-in-law.

Manner of Enslavement: (c) Sold by Relatives or Superiors

Ten of the informants who did not claim they were kidnapped (7%) stated that they were sold by relatives or tribal superiors. Of those who gave details, it is clear that in some cases the victim considered he had been treated badly.

> *Fije, of John Campbell, [a Mahi/EWE] born in the town of Igbege, where he grew up, married two wives, and on his father's death, inherited twenty-two more . . . when he was sold by his uncle because he had not presented him with a female slave and cows on his father's death.*

> *Runago, or Thomas Nicol of Kissy, [a Bidjogo/BIDYOGO] had a child who was just beginning to walk when he was sold by his elder brother to the Portuguese because they could not agree.*

> *Dosu, of John Carew of Freetown, [a Mahi/EWE] . . . had a child about six years old when he was sold by his elder brother on account of a quarrel respecting the property of their father who had been killed in a war against the Dahomeyans. . . .*

Manner of Enslavement: (d) Debt

Ten informants (7%) stated that they had been sold to pay debts, in most cases not of their own contracting. A KAMUKU was sold because of a debt incurred by his father, a butcher: a Baseke/KOTA and a Nki/BOKI were also sold because of paternal debts. Responsibility for debts was considered to extend further than the family circle.

> *Nyamse, or James Hardy of Freetown, [a Bamom/BAMILEKE] . . . lived in Tiapon, a town five days' journey from the capital, to his twenty-fourth year, when he was seized on a trading tour to the Bakoan country, for the debt of another Tiapon man.*

> *Tete, or Frederick Gibbon of Freetown, [an Adampe/EWE] born in the town of Gbotue, where he was married and had a child five years of age,*

when he was seized by the Gaja people, because another Gbotue man, with whom he was in no wise connected, owed them a debt.

Possibly some of those who were "sold by relatives" were sold to pay debts. In rare cases the obligation for the debt was fully accepted by the victim, and one such case is reported by Koelle. The account is moving and deserves to be repeated in full.

Oga, or John Tailor of Freetown, [a Yala/IYALA] born in the town of Gbeku, where he also grew up, married five wives and had thirteen children, eleven of whom died and the eldest of the two remaining was about twenty years of age when a friend sent him to buy a slave, returning with whom they were attacked by a wild cow which killed the slave. The friend then wanted to sell the messenger [i.e., the son] as a restitution for the loss of his slave: but Oga, rather than have his son lose his liberty, offered himself as a slave and was accordingly sold. He was afterwards captured and brought to Sierra Leone, where he has now been twenty years and is the only representative of his tribe. He is now a very old grey-headed man.

Manner of Enslavement: (e) Judicial Process

Persons who were condemned by judicial process in African societies were often enslaved. Sixteen of Koelle's informants (11%) admitted that they had been condemned, and it is likely that some of those who only stated that they had been "sold by relatives" were also, by the laws of their own society, "criminals."

Eleven men . . . had been sold "on account of adultery," a charge which they did not challenge. Two related cases were these:

Asu, or Thomas Harry of Hastings [a Konguang/ANYANG] . . . married two wives, the unfaithfulness of one of whom led him to slay a man, on which account he was sold by the king.

Nanga, or John Smart of Freetown [a Lubalo/KIMBUNDU] born in the town of Mulukala, where he lived to about his twenty-fourth year, when he was given in pawn by his mother for a brother of hers, who had been sold on account of adultery: but before he could be redeemed by his mother, he was placed in the hands of the Portuguese in Loando, who at once shipped him.

Another man, a Melong/MBO was enslaved for murder; an Ihewe/BINI was "sold on a charge of theft"; and a Kanyika/LUBA "had one child which could not walk when he was sold on account of bad conduct." Two men from the Congo coast had been enslaved because of witchcraft accusations.

> *Kumbu, or Thomas Parker of Wilberforce [a Nyombe/KONGO] . . . had a child about five years old, when he was sold because his sister had been accused of witchcraft.*

> *Bembi, or William Davis of Freetown [a Pangela/UMBUNDU] . . . was sold in about his twenty-eighth year because his family had been accused of having occasioned the king's death by means of witchcraft.*

Conclusion

. . . [T]he 179 life-histories here analysed may be claimed to present a miniature of the slave trade within Western tropical Africa in the early nineteenth century, which, though limited in scope and perhaps largely confirmatory of accepted accounts, is well-nigh unique in that it is based solely on information supplied by individual Africans.

Joseph C. Miller

West Central Africa

In his acclaimed account of the Angolan slave trade, Professor Joseph C. Miller of the University of Virginia reconstructs Africans' long, painful, and deadly treks from the deep interior of the continent to the ships awaiting them in the coastal ports. Miller's calculation of the deaths during each stage of the trade is a chilling reminder of the callous losses of human life, although it may be that losses on the way to the coast were lower in other parts of Africa.

. . . The background hunger and epidemics that sometimes forced patrons to give up clients and compelled parents to part with children set a tone of physical weakness and vulnerability behind slaving in the

Joseph C. Miller, "West Central Africa," from The Way of Death, pp. 380–387, 389–391, 398–405, 440–441. Copyright © 1988. Reprinted by permission of The University of Wisconsin Press.

interior. Where warfare and violence stimulated the initial capture, the victims would have begun their odysseys in exhausted, shaken, and perhaps wounded physical condition. Though the buyers preferred strong adult males, the people actually captured in warfare, even in pitched battles between formal armies, included disproportionately high numbers of less fit women and children, since the men could take flight and leave the less mobile retinue of young and female dependents to the pursuers. People sold for food, the last resort in time of famine, also started out physically ill-prepared for the rigors of the journey to come. In the commercialized areas, lords, creditors, and patrons, employing less dramatic methods to seize and sell the dependents who paid for imports or covered their debts, would have selected the least promising among their followings—young boys, older women, the sick, the indebted, the troublesome, and the lame. Populations raided consistently by stronger neighbors, harassed and driven from their homes and fields, and refugee populations hiding on infertile mountaintops could not have been as well-nourished as stronger groups who yielded fewer of their members to the slave trade.

The mixture of people swept off by thousands of isolated decisions and haphazard actions separated into two distinguishable drifts of people. One was a slow, favored one composed principally of the stronger and healthier women and younger children that dissipated into the communities of western central Africa, to remain there as wives and slaves for months or years, or perhaps for life. The debilitated residue became the faster-flowing and sharply defined main channel of people destined for immediate sale and export, victims of drought and raids at the source, joined by small feeder streams of older youths ejected from local communities along its banks as it flowed westward, along with a few women and older folk, and a variety of outcasts and criminals.

The flow headed for the Atlantic coast thus carried weakened individuals relatively vulnerable to disease and death, even by the low health standards of their time. These slaves were not necessarily constitutionally weaker than those left behind or kept but, rather, individuals taken at defenseless and enfeebled moments in their lives. Their temporarily reduced ability to withstand the stresses of enslavement, dislocation, and forced travel could not have failed to produce higher incidences of sickness and death among them than among the population of western central Africa as a whole, even without adding the physical traumas of violent seizure or the psychological shocks of nonviolent enslavement. . . .

These slaves advanced from the hands of their captors, sometimes with periods of rest and partial recuperation in villages along the way, into the market centers where African sellers met European and Luso-African slave-buyers in the interior. People raised in small, dispersed settlements would have encountered the much more volatile disease environments among populations concentrated along the trails, at the staging posts, and finally in the marketplaces themselves. Those from more densely inhabited areas, and even captives who had lived along the roads, encountered new disease environments as they moved into terrain unlike that of their native lands and came into direct contact with foreigners. They would have suffered accordingly from pathogens against which they had no immunities.

The slaves' diets also deteriorated. Whatever plantains, sorghum, or millet they might have eaten at home, supplemented by a healthy variety of game, other crops, and wild plants, as they moved westward they depended increasingly on manioc—the dietary staple that was cheapest to grow, easiest to transport, and most resistant to spoilage—prepared poorly in one form or another. Fresh fruits and vegetables and meat virtually disappeared from their diet. Much of what they were given rotted or became vermin-infested. They were unlikely to have received foods of any sort in quantities sufficient to sustain them, particularly in their weakened conditions, and with vicious circularity they grew too weak to carry what little they were given as they moved. Those who stumbled from weakness were driven onward to keep the remainder moving, all bound together. They drank from inadequate water supplies along the way, sometimes streams, but often not, owing to the tendency of the trails to follow the elevated ridges along the watersheds and the caravan drivers' preference for travel in the dry months. Pools dug out at stopping places were often contaminated from the concentrations of slave caravans that built up around them.

Under such conditions, the slaves developed both dietary imbalances and sheer nutritional insufficiencies. Scurvy, so common among slaves who lived to cross the southern Atlantic that it was known as the *mal de Loanda* (or "Luanda sickness"), was the primary recognized form of undernourishment. The symptoms appeared on slave ships at sea long before they could have developed from shortages of rations on board except among slaves already debilitated by weeks or months of a diet restricted to low vitamin, low acetic acid starches like manioc. With innocent destructiveness some physicians prescribed more manioc as an anti-escorbutic. The slaves who died along the path must have suffered malnutrition to a degree approaching sheer starvation. Racialist Portuguese theories of tropical medicine at the time misdiagnosed the condition, holding that blacks needed to eat less than whites, since they could thrive for days at a time on nothing more than a few millet heads and a kola nut.

The alterations in diet and the amoeba in contaminated water supplies must also have caused the early spread of dysenteries and other intestinal disorders, the infamous "flux" that the British lamented among the slaves they carried across the Atlantic, known as *câmaras* among the Portuguese. Infected excreta left everywhere about water sources, in camp sites, and in the slave pens of the marketplaces assured that few individuals escaped debilitating and dehydrating epidemics of bloody bacillary dysenteries.

Exposure to the dry-season chill in the high elevations and to damp nights spent sitting in open pathside camps, utter lack of clothing and shelter, and increasingly weakened constitutions all contributed to the appearance of respiratory ailments vaguely described as *constipações*. As slaves neared the marketplaces and the main routes running from them down to the coast, they grew weaker and more susceptible to parasites and other diseases that swept in epidemic form through the coffles. The slave trade must have been a veritable incubator for typhus, typhoid, and other fevers or *carneiradas*, particularly smallpox, and other diseases that broke out in times of drought and famine from their usual confinement in the streams of slaves into the general rural population. The normal concentration of these diseases along the commercial routes may have contributed to the impression of overwhelming deadliness that Portuguese held of most of the central African interior, since every European who ventured there necessarily walked within these reservoirs of slave-borne infection on the pathways leading to the interior. . . .

Flight from the slave coffles heading toward the coast, though impossible to estimate precisely in terms of frequency, was not uncommon. Despite the nutritional and epidemiological odds against the slaves, some individuals somehow found the strength to flee their captors. Slaves fled from the marketplaces of the interior, taking refuge among the very people who had just sold them to the Europeans. As they neared the coast, they found willing, though often calculatingly self-interested, asylum among the independent Africans living on either side of Luanda, south of the Kwanza in Kisama, and north of the Dande among the southern Kongo of Musulu. Some fugitives established maroon colonies of their own within Portuguese territory, and there are hints that a major colony of renegades existed throughout the century virtually on the outskirts of Luanda. Some of these colonies had extensive fields and fortifications, including up to forty houses and populations of about 200 people, and lived by raiding Portuguese slave-run plantations in the river valleys. . . .

The slave population entering Luanda was heavily weighted toward younger males by the eighteenth century, reflecting the strain on western central African populations by that time and the widespread resort to debt as means of creating slaves. Older men (*barbados*) also passed through Luanda in significant numbers. Predominant among the women were young females, with a scattering of prime (nubile) women, mothers with infants, and girls, precisely the category of slave that African lords must have been least willing to give up and therefore a further indication of demographic and commercial pressures then bearing on the slave supply zones. . . .

All slaves trembled in terror at meeting the white cannibals of the cities, the first Europeans whom many of the slaves would have seen. They feared the whites' intention of converting Africans' brains into cheese or rendering the fat of African bodies into cooking oil, as well as burning their bones into gunpowder. They clearly regarded the towns as places of certain death, as indeed they became for many, if not for the reasons slaves feared. . . .

The great majority of the slaves went directly to the slave pens of the city's large expatriate merchants. These barracoons—known as *quintais* (singular *quintal*), a word also applied to farmyards for keeping animals—were usually barren enclosures located immediately behind the large two-story residences in the lower town, but traders also constructed them around the edges of the city and on the beach. Large numbers of slaves accumulated within these pens, living for days and weeks surrounded by walls too high for a person to scale, squatting helplessly, naked, on the dirt and entirely exposed to the skies except for a few adjoining cells where they could be locked at night. They lived in a "wormy morass" (*ascarozissimo charco*) and slept in their own excrement, without even a bonfire for warmth. One observer described "two hundred, sometimes three and four hundred slaves in each *quintal*, and there they stayed, ate, slept, and satisfied every human necessity, and from there they infected the houses and the city with the most putrid miasmas; and because dried fish is their usual and preferred food, it was on the walls of these *quintais* and on the roofs of the straw dwellings that such preparation was done, with manifest damage to the public health." To the smell of rotting fish were added the foul odors of the slaves' dysenteries and the putrid fragrance of the bodies of those who died. The stench emanating from these squalid prisons overpowered visitors to the town.

At Benguela the slave pens were about 17 meters square, with walls 3 meters or more in height, and they sometimes contained as many as 150 to 200 slaves, intermixed with pigs and goats also kept in them. That left about two square meters per individual, or barely enough to lie down and to move about a bit. In some instances, at least, the walls had openings cut in them, through which guards outside could thrust musket barrels to fire on slaves within who grew unruly. . . .

The slaves' wait in the barracoons, filthy and unhealthful as it was, leaves the impression of food and water adequate to begin the long process of recuperation from the greater hardships of enslavement and the westward trail. Daily visits to the bay to bathe afforded some slaves an opportunity for limited personal hygiene even amidst the squalor of the slave pens, though they received little that would require cash expenditures by their managers: no clothing, and food barely adequate to sustain them until they would be sold or handed on to the care of the ships' captains waiting to transport them to Brazil. Living conditions for slaves at Benguela would have been worse, owing to the greater shortages of food and water there than in Luanda. But in both ports the sheer opportunity for rest after the rigors of the march from the interior and the availability of salt, iodine, and protein from fish probably allowed the strongest of the young male slaves to recover some of the strength drained from them on their way to the coast. The most penurious merchant could have honestly prided himself on restoring the captives he received toward health, in conformity with his responsibilities to their owners. There may even have been some modest substance to merchants' exaggerated claims that they were doing so. . . .

When the day of the slaves' departure finally dawned, they and their owners and managers set out along yet another tortuous course leading from the slave pens through the long chain of government officials charged with enforcing the maze of rules intended to protect the slaves' bodies and souls and the revenues of the king, though in fact often to the enhancement of none of these. The procedures had been relatively simple earlier in the eighteenth century, but later efforts to curtail tight-packing and smuggling and to improve supplies of food and water aboard the slave ships gradually lengthened the gantlet through which they passed. . . .

. . . Of 100 people seized in Africa, 75 would have reached the marketplaces in the interior; 85 percent of them, or about 64 of the original 100, would have arrived at the coast; after losses of 11 percent in the barracoons, 57 or so would have boarded the ships; of those 57, 51 would have stepped onto Brazilian soil, and 48 or 49 would have lived to behold their first master in the New World. The full "seasoning" period of 3–4 years would leave only 28 or 30 of the original 100 alive and working. A total "wastage" factor of about two-thirds may thus be estimated for the late-eighteenth-century Angolan trade, higher earlier in the trade, probably a bit lower by the 1820s, with slaves from the wetter equatorial latitudes always showing a lower mortality rate than those from Luanda and Benguela. As such, even at that late date it was a number amply large to rivet the fatalistic attention of the slavers in the Angolan trade and the merchants supporting them, to force all involved to stress speed, and to prompt the wealthy and powerful to organize its financial structures so as to avoid, where they could, the risks and costs resulting from mortality they could not control. It was literally, and sadly, true that "if few die the profit is certain, but if many are lost so also is their owner."

Joseph E. Inikori

Guns for Slaves

Nigerian-born Joseph E. Inikori, a historian at the University of Rochester, examines the flow of firearms into Africa in exchange for slaves. While stressing that African demand largely determined the quantity and quality of weaponry imported, he also argues that firearm imports stimulated warfare to obtain the slaves that paid for the guns.

Joseph E. Inikori, "Guns for Slaves" from "The Import of Firearms into West Africa," *Journal of African History*, 18.3, 1977, pp. 340–341, 343, 345–346, 348–351, 361–362. Reprinted by permission of Cambridge University Press.

The very high demand for guns which prevailed in West Africa in the eighteenth century is reflected in the fact that £1 sterling of guns had a much greater purchasing power in West Africa than £1 sterling of other goods. . . . The general pressure on gun manufacturers whenever the volume of English trade to West Africa was on the increase is a further proof of the great demand for guns in the trade. . . . It was not for nothing, therefore, that while the bill to abolish the slave trade was being debated in the British parliament, the gun manufacturers in and around Birmingham petitioned the House of Commons that the abolition of the slave trade would be extremely detrimental to them, because "by such abolition the greatest, and perhaps only, efficient nursery for artificers in the art of manufacturing of arms, would be destroyed."

But, important as firearms and ammunition were in West African trade at this time, we have no estimates of the quantities annually imported over particular periods. . . . Very fortunately, the account prepared for the British House of Commons in 1806 by William Irving, the Inspector General of Imports and Exports of Great Britain, shows the official and real values of ordnance and small arms exported from England to the coast of Africa for ten years, 1796–1805. Private records of English merchants trading to the coast of Africa show the prices of various types of guns (6,530 in all) exported to the African coast over the same period. From this the average price of guns exported from England to West Africa during this period has been calculated. . . . This average price has been used . . . to compute the number of guns annually exported from England to the coast of Africa. . . .

This calculation shows that between 1796 and 1805 a total of 1,615,309 guns were imported into West Africa from England, giving an annual average of 161,531. This may be compared with the statement made in 1765 by Lord Shelburne, that Birmingham alone had been sending more than 150,000 guns yearly to the African coast during the preceding twenty or twenty-five years. Taking into account quantities made in other parts of England (in particular Liverpool, Bristol and London) and sent to the African coast, Shelburne's statement could be interpreted to mean that about 200,000 guns were exported annually from England to the coast of Africa from the 1740s to 1765. . . .

The available evidence points to the fact that the other European countries who traded to the West Coast of Africa expended, at least, as many guns per unit of payment for goods purchased as the English.

Therefore, the figures of imports from England can be used to estimate total imports from all parts, based on England's share of the total trade. . . . While some margin of error should be expected, the share of the total trade held by English merchants suggested by these figures, about 45 percent, may not be far from the mark, either way. Using this share with the import figures from England gives something between 444,000 and 333,000 as the total number of guns annually imported into the West Coast of Africa in the second half of the eighteenth century. . . .

The use to which the firearms imported were put seems to be the most controversial issue relating to firearms in Africa. At one time it was suggested that the firearms were "ostensibly for decorating the habitation of some Negro chieftain." This was refuted in 1790 by Alexander Falconbridge. Asked by a committee of enquiry whether he had "ever observed in the houses of any of the chiefs or great men, guns in a considerable number, as if kept for the purpose of show or ornament," he replied that "I have seen a great number in their houses with different kinds of goods, which I always understood were for trade," speaking particularly of Bonny where he had been more on shore than any other place.

More recently, it has been suggested that the most important use to which firearms were put in Africa was the protection of crops, the introduction of Indian corn being related to firearms. Other writers argue that the introduction of firearms into Africa represented an important technical innovation in slave gathering, the imported firearms being used primarily for raids and wars directed to the acquisition of captives for sale. . . .

The strong preference of the slave sellers for guns indicates very strongly the connexion between firearms and the acquisition of slaves. It reinforces the slave gun cycle theory according to which the states and individual or groups of individual slave gatherers bought more firearms to capture more slaves to buy more firearms. . . . For some states the necessity may have been imposed by defence requirements. But for the professional slave gatherers the firearms represented important inputs.

This is not to say, however, that the guns acquired through the sale of slaves were employed solely for the gathering of slaves. The private slave gatherer who purchased firearms for that purpose may have at the same time used his private materials in time of need to fight the wars of the state, the clan, the village, etc.—wars of aggression, retaliation or defence, unconnected or only indirectly connected with slaving. Where slave gathering was a state affair, the slave-gathering state may not only have waged offensive wars calculated for the capture of slaves. Its slave-gathering activities would of necessity provoke attack by its neighbours and so be forced to defend itself. On the other hand, the "non-slaving" states that acquired large quantities of firearms through the sale of slaves did so in order to be able to defend themselves effectively against the onslaught of slave-gathering states and others. Because slave-gathering by its very nature provoked inter-territorial wars in different ways, in addition to inter-territorial conflicts arising from other causes, firearms acquired for slave-gathering or for defence against slave-gatherers may have been employed in a host of operations not directly connected with slave-gathering. And, for that matter, firearms purchased for slave-gathering and/or military purposes may also have been put to peaceful uses at the same time by the possessors, particularly for hunting and firing during ceremonial occasions. . . .

The implication of all this is that the firearms imported into West Africa in the second half of the eighteenth century were used mainly for slave-gathering and the wars largely stimulated by the latter. This is why the most important slave exporting areas of the time, in particular, the Bonny trading area, were also the largest firearms importers in West Africa during this period. Not only did the Bonny trading area import more guns absolutely than other parts of West Africa, but also, it imported far more guns for every slave exported. Whereas the observations of contemporaries on the low quality of the firearms imported into West Africa are generally supported by the evidence, they contain a great deal of exaggeration. A large proportion of the firearms were very much better than the contemporary observers would want us to believe. What is important, however, is that the firearms seem largely to have served the purpose for which the African buyers purchased them. If this were not the case, firearms which were more efficient in meeting slave sellers' needs would have been brought to the coast in the face of the keen competition for slaves by the European merchants in the second half of the eighteenth century. It is remarkable, indeed, that the most important slave exporting area of this period, Bonny, tended to import more of the cheaper and low quality types of guns. Finally, it seems likely that the use to which firearms imported were put in West Africa changed over time. It is most likely that hunting became the most important employment of firearms after 1900.

John Thornton

Warfare and Slavery

In his widely read and influential study of Africans in the Atlantic world, John Thornton rejects the notion that a guns-for-slaves cycle drove the movement of slaves to the coast. Basing his argument on the nature of African warfare and the size of African states, Thornton relies heavily on the existence of large slave populations *within* African societies. Thus, his argument resembles that of Mungo Park two centuries earlier.

We have established so far that Africans were not under any direct commercial or economic pressure to deal in slaves. Furthermore, we have seen not only that Africans accepted the institution of slavery in their own societies, but that the special place of slaves as private productive property made slavery widespread. At the beginning, at least, Europeans were only tapping existing slave markets. Nevertheless, one need not accept that these factors alone can explain the slave trade. There are scholars who contend that although Europeans did not invade the continent and take slaves themselves, they did nevertheless promote the slave trade through indirect military pressure created by European control of important military technology, such as horses and guns. In this scenario—the "gun–slave cycle" or "horse–slave cycle"—Africans were compelled to trade in slaves, because without this commerce they could not obtain the necessary military technology (guns or horses) to defend themselves from any enemy. Furthermore, possession of the technology made them more capable of obtaining slaves, because successful war guaranteed large supplies of slaves.

Hence, through the operation of their control over the "means of destruction," . . . Europeans were able to influence Africans indirectly. They could direct commerce in ways that helped them and also compel Africans to wage wars that might otherwise not have been waged. This would cause Africans to seek more slaves than they needed for their own political and economic ends and depopulate the country against their

John Thornton, "Warfare and Slavery," from *Africa and Africans in the Making of the Atlantic World, 1400–1800*, 1992, 1998, pp. 98–102, 104–108, 110, 112–114, 116–117, 119–120, 125. Reprinted by permission of Cambridge University Press.

wishes. The quantitative increase would exceed Africans' own judgment of a proper level of exports. In the end, this not only might increase economic dependence but could result in large-scale destruction of goods, tools, and ultimately development potential. Hence, in the end, Africans would be helpless, exploited junior partners in a commerce directed by Europe.

However, this argument will ultimately not be any more sustainable than the earlier commercial and economic ones. Certainly in the period before 1680, European technology was not essential for warfare, even if Africans did accept some of it. Likewise, it is much easier to assert than to demonstrate that Africans went to war against their will or solely to service the slave trade. Indeed the more we know about African warfare and resulting enslavement, the less clear and direct the connections between war and the export slave trade become.

The contemporary evidence strongly supports the idea that there was a direct connection between wars and slavery, both for domestic work and for export. . . .

Thus the fact that military enslavement was by far the most significant method is important, for it means that rulers were not, for the most part, selling their own subjects but people whom they, at least, regarded as aliens. The fact that many exported slaves were recent captives means that they were drawn from those captured in the course of warfare who had not yet been given an alternative employment within Africa. In these cases, rulers were deciding to forgo the potential future use of these slaves. Some of the exports were slaves whom local masters wished to dispose of for one reason or another and those who had been captured locally by brigands or judicially enslaved. . . .

The causes and motivations behind these wars are crucial for understanding the slave trade. Philip Curtin has examined the Senegambian slave trade of the eighteenth century and has proposed a schema for viewing African warfare that resulted in slave captures that can be fruitfully applied to the earlier period as well. He proposes that wars be classified as tending toward either an economic or a political model. In the economic model the wars were fought for the express purpose of acquiring slaves and perhaps to meet demands from European merchants; in the political model wars were fought for mostly political reasons, and slaves were simply a by-product that might yield a profit. Both models are seen as "ideal types," and individual wars might contain a mixture of motives, of course. On the whole, however, Curtin believes that the eighteenth-century Senegambian data support a political, rather than the economic, model.

Actually, discerning between an economic and a political model is not easy in practice. . . . This issue goes to the heart of the unusual nature of African politics and one of the matters that makes it different from Eurasian politics. Just as slavery took the place of landed property in Africa, so slave raids were equivalent to wars of conquest. For this reason, one must apply a different logic to African wars than the equations of political motives equals war of conquest and economic motives equals slave raid. This analysis changes our understanding of the objectives of war and must ultimately change our assessment of African warfare.

[Paul] Lovejoy, for example, has proposed that warfare was endemic in Africa as a result of political fragmentation. In other words, the very fact that Africa had few large-scale political units meant that wars would be more frequent, and thus enslavement increased. As fragmentation increased (a situation that he believes took place during the period of the slave trade), war naturally increased. Underlying this is the assumption that a political situation of small states would naturally lead to a movement to consolidate them into larger, Eurasian-style polities. Thus, although African politics actually determined the course of warfare, the intrinsic structure of those politics created more wars. Furthermore, one need not consider most wars as being explained by the economic model but by the political model, in which wars were an attempt to remedy the fragmentation by consolidating power. The failure to consolidate was thus the fuel that fired the slave trade.

Lovejoy's solution would be more helpful if it were true that there is a correlation between political centralization and peace, but unfortunately this does not seem to have been the case. . . .

In all, only perhaps 30 percent of Atlantic Africa's area was occupied by states with surface areas larger than 50,000 square kilometers, and at least half of that area was occupied by states in the medium-sized (50,000–150,000 square kilometers) range. The rest of Atlantic Africa was occupied by small, even tiny, states. . . . [B]roken down by population, a portion considerably greater than half of all the people in Atlantic Africa lived in the ministates, because these states were found in the most densely populated parts of the region.

Thus, one can say with confidence that political fragmentation was the norm in Atlantic Africa. By this account, the "typical" Atlantic African probably lived in a state that had absolute sovereignty but controlled a territory not exceeding 1,500 square kilometers (smaller than many American counties, perhaps the area occupied by a larger city). Populations might vary considerably; in the sparsely inhabited areas of central Africa, such a state might have 3,000–5,000 inhabitants, but on the densely inhabited Slave and Gold coasts it could control as many as 20,000–30,000 people. Virtually all the land from the Gambia River along the coast to the Niger delta was in states of this size, and much of the land stretching into the interior. In areas like Angola, ministates like these occupied the mountainous land between Kongo and Ndongo and the area of the Kwanza River between Ndongo and the larger states of the central highlands.

In short, enlargement of scale does not seem to have been a priority for leaders. Historians, anxious to assert that Africans did build large states, have to some extent focused too much attention on the empires and the medium-sized states, and thus the point is often overlooked. But the reasons for Africa's small states were probably not the result of some sort of backwardness that prevented them from seeing the advantages of larger units.

One reason for the smallness of scale (not necessarily the only one) may derive from the legal system, which did not make land private property, and may also explain why the Americas, the other world area without landed property, was also the home of small and even tiny states (outside its own few dramatic empires). In Eurasia, control over large areas of land was essential, because it was through grants of land that one rewarded followers, and this land was normally worked by tenants of one kind or another. Eurasians were relatively less interested in controlling people, for without land, the people's labor could not be assigned or its reward collected by landowners. African states were not concerned with land— for as long as there was no population pressure on the land, more people could always be accommodated. Hence, African wars that aimed at acquiring slaves were in fact the exact equivalent of Eurasian wars aimed at acquiring land. The state and its citizens could increase their wealth by acquiring slaves and did not need to acquire land, unless they were short of land at home (which was not the case, as far as we can tell).

The acquisition of slaves instead of land in wars had other advantages. Whereas conquest of land necessarily required administration of larger areas and expansion of military resources, the acquisition of slaves only required a short campaign that need not create any new administrative conditions. Moreover, conquest of land and its subsequent government usually required sharing the proceeds of land with existing landlords, state officials, and other wealthy members of the defeated state, who might be defeated but usually still had to be co-opted. Slaves, on the other hand, were unable to bargain as wealthy landlords might have and could be integrated individually or in small groups into existing structures. . . . Many Africans retained females from the raids and sold off males, because the Atlantic trade often demanded more males than females. . . .

Increasing wealth through warfare and enslavement was of course a cheap way of increasing power. Slaves could be captured in wars and in raids and carried back to the home territory by the victors and put to work, without the attacking armies having to conquer and occupy territory. For small states with small armies, this was a logical way to become richer. But of course, in the medium-sized states and empires, territorial expansion also took place. . . . [E]nslavement of the conquered population allowed the rulers of the expanding state to increase their personal wealth and also to build armies and administrative corps of direct dependents, just as the revenues from the conquered territories provided continuous new income. Thus, external expansion could also increase wealth, and the slaves that were a by-product of the wars of expansion could increase centralization at home.

All these factors resulted in an enormous slave population in Africa at the time of the arrival of the first Europeans and during the whole era of the slave trade. They meant that the necessary legal institutions and material resources were available to support a large slave market, one that anyone could participate in, including Europeans and other foreigners. Those who held slaves and did not intend to use them immediately could also sell them, and indeed, this is why the number of African merchants who dealt in slaves was large. . . .

This interpretation of African politics has reemphasized the importance of domestic slavery in Africa. Obviously, slaves were sufficiently important that one could find many in African societies. Likewise, as we have suggested, exports tended to be drawn from those slaves who were recently captured and had not yet found a place in the society of their enslavers. This aspect of slavery obviously places emphasis on the African decisions concerning which slaves to sell to Europeans and when. These decisions were in turn a product of the specific situation in each country, including price and availability of slaves. In large measure, the decision to participate in the Atlantic trade required that specific conditions be met, and countries often entered and left the trade. . . .

Although I have shown that African wars led to enslavement on a large scale and that African politics can explain even slaves raids that seem to have no political motive, the hypothesis that Europeans influenced African behavior through control over military resources must still be addressed. Given the significance of warfare for expansion of wealth in Africa, the military case must be carefully examined.

Certainly, Europeans did participate, wherever possible, in African politics, often as "military experts" or advisors, occasionally as armed mercenaries. They did this both officially through government-sponsored assistance programs, such as the aid that Portugal gave to Kongo in 1491, 1509, 1512, and 1570, or unofficially and without authorization, as in the support for Ndongo in the 1520s, the help that gunners gave to the Mane in the 1550s, and perhaps the assistance to Benin in the 1510s and 1520s. Other foreigners of European origin also provided assistance—Hawkins's help in Sierra Leone and Ulsheimer's in Benin are two more sixteenth- and early seventeenth-century examples. Acceptance of this assistance might simply be seen as the desire of centralizers to make use of foreign, rather than local, officials and dependents as a means of keeping local political debts to a minimum and of creating a dependent bureaucracy. But it is also clear that Europeans provided new military techniques and technology as well, perhaps at the price of demanding more vigorous participation in the slave trade than their patrons wished.

However, the kind of military assistance that Europeans in the sixteenth and seventeenth centuries could render in Africa was not as decisive as much of the writing on the "gun–slave" and "horse–slave" cycles implies. . . . European firearms and crossbows, the missile weapons that differed most from those in use in Africa, were designed to counteract armored cavalry or for naval warfare in Europe. Although they had great range and penetrating power (capabilities that developed out of a long-standing projectile-versus-armor contest), they had a very slow rate of fire. For Africans, who generally eschewed armor, the advantages of range (penetrating power being relatively unimportant) were more than offset by the disadvantages of the slow rate of fire, except in special circumstances. . . .

In summary, we can say that although European arms may have assisted African rulers in war in some cases, they were not decisive. It is unlikely that any European technology or assistance increased the Africans' chances of waging successful war (as the Portuguese in Angola could surely have attested) or that it made the attackers suffer fewer losses. Therefore, Europeans did not bring about some sort of military revolution that forced participation in the Atlantic trade as a price for survival. . . .

PART

III The Middle
Passage

================= VARIETY OF OPINION =================

We were thrust into the hold in a state of nudity . . . ; the hold was so low we could not stand up. . . .

MAHOMMAH GARDO BAQUAQUA

Here we have nearly one-third given apparently for the average loss on the passage, and this estimated by the slave-dealers themselves on the American side of the Atlantic.

THOMAS FOWELL BUXTON

One conclusion that might be drawn is that, in reducing the estimated total export of slaves from about twenty million to about ten million, the harm done to African societies is also reduced by half. This is obvious nonsense.

PHILIP D. CURTIN

Thousands of ship crossings have now been statistically analyzed, and none show a correlation of any significance between either tonnage or space available and mortality.

HERBERT S. KLEIN

The evidential base for the study of the Atlantic slave trade . . . has been revolutionized. . . . Perhaps this book will be the last to devote a major part of its thrust to assessing the overall size of the slave trade.

DAVID ELTIS AND DAVID RICHARDSON

Mahommah Gardo Baquaqua

An African's Ordeal

Few Africans who crossed the Atlantic on a slave ship had both the opportunity and the desire to write of their experiences. One who did was Mahommah G. Baquaqua, who was sold from the infamous port of Whydah on the Slave Coast in the 1840s. Though his autobiography is less well known than that of Olaudah Equiano, modern scholars have confirmed the authenticity of Baquaqua's account of the Middle Passage whereas Equiano's has been questioned. Both authors emphasized the physical and mental ordeals of their Atlantic voyages.

When all were ready to go aboard, we were chained together, and tied with ropes round about our necks, and were thus drawn down to the sea shore. The ship was lying some distance off. I had never seen a ship before, and my idea of it was, that it was some object of worship of the white man. I imagined that we were all to be slaughtered, and

From Samuel Moore, "Biography of Mahommah G. Baquaqua, a Native of Zoogoo, in the Interior of Africa" (Detroit: Geo. E. Pomeroy & Co., 1854), p. 41–44. Printed from the electronic edition in "Documenting the American South," Copyright © 2001, University of North Carolina, Chapel Hill.

AN INTERESTING NARRATIVE.

BIOGRAPHY

OF

MAHOMMAH G. BAQUAQUA,

A NATIVE OF ZOOGO, IN THE INTERIOR OF AFRICA.

(A Convert to Christianity,)

WITH A DESCRIPTION OF THAT PART OF THE WORLD;

INCLUDING THE

Manners and Customs of the Inhabitants,

Their Religious Notions, Form of Government, Laws, Appearance of the Country, Buildings, Agriculture, Manufactures, Shepherds and Herdsmen, Animals, Marriage and Funeral Ceremonies, Dress, Trade and Commerce, Warfare, Slavery, with an Account of Mahommah's captivity, Education, Capture and Slavery in Africa and Brazil, Escape, Reception by Rev. W. L. Judd, Baptist Missionary at Port au Prince, Conversion to Christianity, Baptism, his Views, Objects and Aim, &c.

WRITTEN AND REVISED FROM HIS OWN WORDS,

BY SAMUEL MOORE, ESQ.,

Late publisher of the "North of England Shipping Gazette," author of several popular works, and editor of sundry reform papers.

MAHOMMAH G. BAQUAQUA.

Engraved by J. C. Darby, from a Daguerreotype by Dalton.

DETROIT:

Printed for the Author, Mahommah Gardo Baquaqua,

BY GEO. E. POMEROY & CO., TRIBUNE OFFICE.

1854.

Biography of Mahommah G. Baquaqua written and revised from his own words, by
Samuel Moore (Detroit, 1854), title page. (Library of Congress)

were being led there for that purpose. I felt alarmed for my safety, and despondency had almost taken sole possession of me.

A kind of feast was made ashore that day, and those who rowed the boats were plentifully regaled with whiskey, and the slaves were given rice and other good things in abundance. I was not aware that it was to be my last feast in Africa. I did not know my destiny. Happy for me, that I did not. All I knew was, that I was a slave, chained by the neck, and that I must readily and willingly submit, come what would, which I considered was as much as I had any right to know.

At length, when we reached the beach, and stood on the sand, oh! how I wished that the sand would open and swallow me up. My wretchedness I cannot describe. It was beyond description. The reader may imagine, but anything like an outline of my feelings would fall very short of the mark, indeed. There were slaves brought hither from all parts of the country, and taken on board the ship. The first boat had reached the vessel in safety, notwithstanding the high wind and rough sea; but the last boat that ventured was upset, and all in her but one man were drowned. The number who were lost was about thirty. The man that was saved was very stout, and stood at the head of the boat with a chain in his hand, which he grasped very tightly in order to steady the boat; and when the boat turned over, he was thrown with the rest into the sea, but on rising, by some means under the boat, managed to turn it over, and thus saved himself by springing into her, when she righted. This required great strength, and being a powerful man gave him the advantage over the rest. The next boat that was put to sea, I was placed in; but God saw fit to spare me, perhaps for some good purpose. I was then placed in that most horrible of all places, THE SLAVE SHIP.

Its horrors, ah! who can describe? None can so truly depict its horrors as the poor unfortunate, miserable wretch that has been confined within its portals. Oh! friends of humanity, pity the poor African, who has been trepanned and sold away from friends and home, and consigned to the hold of a slave ship, to await even more horrors and miseries in a distant land, amongst the religious and benevolent. Yes, even in their very midst; but to the ship! We were thrust into the hold of the vessel in a state of nudity, the males being crammed on one side and the females on the other; the hold was so low that we could not stand up, but were obliged to crouch upon the floor or sit down; day and night were the same to us, sleep being denied as from the confined position of our bodies, and we became desperate through suffering and fatigue.

Oh! the loathsomeness and filth of that horrible place will never be effaced from my memory; nay, as long as memory holds her seat in this distracted brain, will I remember that. My heart even at this day, sickens at the thought of it.

Let those humane individuals, who are in favor of slavery, only allow themselves to take the slave's position in the noisome hold of a slave ship, just for one trip from Africa to America, and without going into the horrors of slavery further than this, if they do not come out thorough-going abolitionists, then I have no more to say in favor of abolition. But I think their views and feelings regarding slavery will be changed in some degree, however; if not, let them continue in the course of slavery, and work out their term in a cotton or rice field, or other plantation, and then if they do not say hold, enough! I think they must be of iron frames, possessing neither hearts nor souls. I imagine there can be but one place more horrible in all creation than the hold of a slave ship, and that place is where slaveholders and their myrmidons are the most likely to find themselves some day, when alas, 'twill be too late, too late, alas!

The only food we had during the voyage was corn soaked and boiled. I cannot tell how long we were thus confined, but it seemed a very long while. We suffered very much for want of water, but was denied all we needed. A pint a day was all that was allowed, and no more; and a great many slaves died upon the passage. There was one poor fellow became so very desperate for want of water, that he attempted to snatch a knife from the white man who brought in the water, when he was taken up on deck and I never knew what became of him. I supposed he was thrown overboard.

When any one of us became refractory, his flesh was cut with a knife, and pepper or vinegar was rubbed in to make him peaceable(!) I suffered, and so did the rest of us, very much from sea sickness at first, but that did not cause our brutal owners any trouble. Our sufferings were our own, we had no one to share our troubles, none to care for us, or even to speak a word of comfort to us. Some were thrown overboard before breath was out of their bodies, when it was thought any would not live, they were got rid of in that way. Only twice during the voyage were we allowed to go on deck to wash ourselves—once whilst at sea, and again just before going into port.

We arrived at Pernambuco, South America, early in the morning, and the vessel played about during the day, without coming to anchor. All that day we neither ate or drank anything, and we were given to understand that we were to remain perfectly silent, and not make any out-cry, otherwise our lives were in danger. But when "night threw her sable mantle on the earth and sea," the anchor dropped, and we were permitted to go on deck to be viewed and handled by our future masters, who had come aboard from the city. We landed a few miles from the city, at a farmer's house, which was used as a kind of slave market. The farmer had a great many slaves, and I had not been there very long before I saw him use the lash pretty freely on a boy, which made a deep impression on my mind, as of course I imagined that would be my fate ere long, and oh! too soon, alas! were my fears realized.

When I reached the shore, I felt thankful to Providence that I was once more permitted to breathe pure air, the thought of which almost absorbed every other. I cared but little then that I was a slave, having escaped the ship was all I thought about. Some of the slaves on board could talk Portuguese. They had been living on the coast with Portuguese families, and they used to interpret to us. They were not placed in the hold with the rest of us, but come down occasionally to tell us something or other.

These slaves never knew they were to be sent away, until they were placed on board the ship. I remained in this slave market but a day or two, before I was again sold to a slave dealer in the city, who again sold me to a man in the country, who was a baker, and resided not a great distance from Pernambuco.

Thomas Fowell Buxton

An Abolitionist's Evidence

Sir Thomas Fowell Buxton was a member of the British Parliament who turned his attention from domestic prison reform to the abolition of the slave trade. His major work, the *African Slave Trade*, was published in 1839, long after Britain had ceased carrying slaves but before other nations had done so. The grisly details of the slave trade Buxton gleaned from eyewitnesses and official sources were meant to keep up pressure on governments to end the trade.

From Thomas Fowell Buxton, *The Atlantic Slave Trade and Its Remedy* (London, 1840), pp. 122, 124–133, 135–139, 172–175.

It was well observed by Mr. Fox, in a debate on the Slave Trade, that

> *True humanity consists not in a squeamish ear; it consists not in starting or shrinking at such tales as these, but in a disposition of heart to relieve misery. True humanity appertains rather to the mind than to the nerves, and prompts men to use real and active endeavours to execute the actions which it suggests.*

In the spirit of this observation, I now go on to remark, that the first feature of this deadly passage, which attracts our attention, is the evident insufficiency, in point of tonnage, of the vessels employed, for the cargoes of human beings which they are made to contain. . . .

We have a faithful description of the miseries of the middle passage, from the pen of an eye-witness, Mr. Falconbridge. His account refers to a period antecedent to 1790. He tells us that

> *The men Negroes, on being brought aboard ship, are immediately fastened together two and two, by handcuffs on their wrists, and by irons riveted on their legs. . . . They are frequently stowed so close as to admit of no other posture than lying on their sides. Neither will the height between decks, unless directly under the grating, permit them the indulgence of an erect posture, especially where there are platforms, which is generally the case. These platforms are a kind of shelf, about eight or nine feet in breadth, extending from the side of the ship towards the center. They are placed nearly midway between the decks, at the distance of two or three feet from each deck. Upon these the Negroes are stowed in the same manner as they are on the deck underneath.*

After mentioning some other arrangements, he goes on to say,

> *It often happens that those who are placed at a distance from the buckets, in endeavouring to get to them, tumble over their companions, in consequence of their being shackled. These accidents, although unavoidable, are productive of continual quarrels, in which some of them are always bruised. In this distressed situation they desist from the attempt, and . . . this becomes a fresh source of broils and disturbances, and tends to render the situation of the poor captive wretches still more uncomfortable.*

> *In favourable weather they are fed upon deck, but in bad weather their food is given to them below. Numberless quarrels take place among them during their meals; more especially when they are put upon short allowance, which frequently happens. In that case, the weak are obliged to*

be content with a very scanty portion. Their allowance of water is about half a pint each, at every meal.

Upon the negroes refusing to take sustenance, I have seen coals of fire, glowing hot, put on a shovel, and placed so near their lips as to scorch and burn them, and this has been accompanied with threats of forcing them to swallow the coals, if they any longer persisted in refusing to eat. These means have generally the desired effect. I have also been credibly informed that a certain captain in the Slave Trade poured melted lead on such of the negroes as obstinately refused their food.

Falconbridge then tells us that the negroes are sometimes compelled to dance and to sing, and that, if any reluctance is exhibited, the cat-o'-nine-tails is employed to enforce obedience. He goes on to mention the unbounded licence given to the officers and crew of the slavers, as regards the women; and, speaking of the officers, he says, they

are sometimes guilty of such brutal excesses as disgrace human nature. . . . But, . . . the hardships and inconveniences suffered by the negroes during the passage are scarcely to be enumerated or conceived. They are far more violently affected by the sea-sickness than the Europeans. It frequently terminates in death, especially among the women. The exclusion of the fresh air is among the most intolerable. Most ships have air-ports; but, whenever the sea is rough and the rain heavy, it becomes necessary to shut these and every other conveyance by which air is admitted. The fresh air being thus excluded, the negroes' rooms very soon grow intolerably hot. The confined air, rendered noxious by the effluvia exhaled from their bodies, and by being repeatedly breathed, soon produces fevers and fluxes, which generally carry off great numbers of them. During the voyages I made, I was frequently a witness to the fatal effects of this exclusion of the fresh air. I will give one instance, as it serves to convey some idea, though a very faint one, of the state of these unhappy beings. Some wet and blowing weather having occasioned the portholes to be shut, and the gratings to be covered, fluxes and fevers among the negroes ensued. My profession requiring it, I frequently went down among them, till at length their apartments became so extremely hot as to be only sufferable for a very short time. But the excessive heat was not the only thing that rendered their situation intolerable. The deck, that is, the floor of their rooms, was so covered with the blood and mucus which had proceeded from them in consequence of the flux, that it resembled a slaughter-house. It is not in the power of human imagination to picture to itself a situation more dreadful or more disgusting. . . .

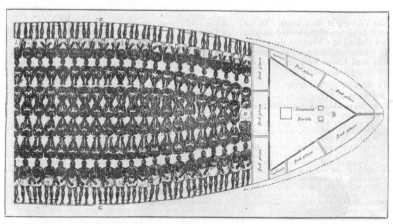

Slave Transport, circa 1750, A diagram showing how slaves were packed into the hull of a ship, some standing, some sitting. (Illustration source unknown/Photo by Henry Guttmann/Getty Images)

He proceeds to notice the case of a Liverpool vessel which took on board at the Bonny River nearly 700 slaves (more than three to each ton!); and Falconbridge says,

> By purchasing so great a number, the slaves were so crowded, that they were even obliged to lie one upon another. This occasioned such a mortality among them, that, without meeting with unusual bad weather, or having a longer voyage than common, nearly one-half of them died before the ship arrived in the West Indies.

He then describes the treatment of the sick as follows:

> The place allotted for the sick negroes is under the half-deck, where they lie on the bare plank. By this means, those who are emaciated frequently have their skin, and even their flesh, entirely rubbed off, by the motion of the ship, from the prominent parts of the shoulders, elbows, and hips, so as to render the bones in those parts quite bare. The excruciating pain which the poor sufferers feel from being obliged to continue in so dreadful a situation, frequently for several weeks, in case they happen to live so long, is not to be conceived or described. Few indeed are ever able to withstand the fatal effects of it. The surgeon, upon going between decks in the morning, frequently finds several of the slaves dead, and, among the men, sometimes a dead and a living negro fastened by their irons together.

He then states that surgeons are driven to engage in the "Guinea Trade" by the confined state of their finances; and that, at most, the only way in which a surgeon can render himself useful, is by seeing that the food is properly cooked and distributed to the slaves:

> *When once the fever and dysentery get to any height at sea, a cure is scarcely ever effected.*

> *One-half, sometimes two-thirds, and even beyond that, have been known to perish. Before we left Bonny River no less than fifteen died of fevers, and dysenteries, occasioned by their confinement.*

Falconbridge also told the Committee of 1790, that,

> *in stowing the slaves, they wedge them in, so that they had not as much room as a man in his coffin: that, when going from one side of their rooms to the other, he always took off his shoes, but could not avoid pinching them; and that he had the marks on his feet where they bit and scratched him. Their confinement in this situation was so injurious, that he has known them to go down apparently in good health at night, and be found dead in the morning.*

Any comment on the statement of Falconbridge must be superfluous: he had been a surgeon in slave-ships, he was a respectable witness before the Committee of Inquiry in 1790, and gave the substance of this statement in evidence. And it ought to be borne in mind that he was an eye-witness of the scenes which he has described. His evidence is the more valuable, when it is considered that we have long been debarred from testimony equally credible and direct: as, since 1807, Britain has taken no part in the slave-traffic; and it has been the policy of the foreign nations who have continued the trade to conceal, as far as they could, the horrors and miseries which are its attendants.

Mr. Granville Sharpe (the zealous advocate of the negro) brought forward a case which aroused public attention to the horrors of this passage. In his Memoirs we have the following account taken from his private memoranda:

> *March 19, 1783. Gustavus Vas[s]a called on me with an account of 132 negroes being thrown alive into the sea, from on board an English slave-ship.*

> *The circumstances of this case could not fail to excite a deep interest. The master of a slave-ship trading from Africa to Jamaica, and having*

440 *slaves on board, had thought fit, on a pretext that he might be distressed on his voyage for want of water, to lessen the consumption of it in the vessel, by throwing overboard* 132 *of the most sickly among the slaves. On his return to England, the owners of the ship claimed from the in surers the full value of those drowned slaves, on the ground that there was an absolute necessity for throwing them into the sea, in order to save the remaining crew, and the ship itself. The underwriters contested the existence of the alleged necessity; or, if it had existed, attributed it to the ignorance and improper conduct of the master of the vessel. This contest of pecuniary interest brought to light a scene of horrid brutality which had been acted during the execution of a detestable plot. From the trial it appeared that the ship* Zong, *Luke Collingwood master, sailed from the island of St. Thomas, on the coast of Africa, September 6, 1781, with* 440 *slaves and fourteen whites on board, for Jamaica, and that in the November following she fell in with that island; but, instead of proceeding to some port, the master, mistaking, as he alleges, Jamaica for Hispaniola, ran her to leeward. Sickness and mortality had by this time taken place on board the crowded vessel: so that, between the time of leaving the coast of Africa and the* 29th *of November, sixty slaves and seven white people had died; and a great number of the surviving slaves were then sick and not likely to live. On that day the master of the ship called together a few of the officers, and stated to them that, if the sick slaves died a natural death, the loss would fall on the owners of the ship; but, if they were thrown alive into the sea, on any sufficient pretext of necessity for the safety of the ship, it would be the loss of the underwriters, alleging, at the same time, that it would be less cruel to throw sick wretches into the sea, than to suffer them to linger out a few days under the disorder with which they were afflicted.*

To *this inhuman proposal the mate, James Kelsal, at first objected; but Collingwood at length prevailed on the crew to listen to it. He then chose out from the cargo* 132 *slaves, and brought them on deck, all or most of whom were sickly, and not likely to recover, and he ordered the crew by turns to throw them into the sea. "A parcel" of them were accordingly thrown overboard, and, on counting over the remainder the next morning, it appeared that the number so drowned had been fifty-four. He then ordered another parcel to be thrown over, which, on a second counting on the succeeding day, was proved to have amounted to forty-two.*

On *the third day the remaining thirty-six were brought on deck, and, as these now resisted the cruel purpose of their masters, the arms of twenty-six were fettered with irons, and the savage crew proceeded with the diabolical work, casting them down to join their comrades of the former days. Outraged misery could endure no longer; the ten last victims sprang disdainfully from the grasp of their tyrants, defied their power, and, leaping into the sea, felt a momentary triumph in the embrace of death. . . .*

Such were some of the cruelties of the middle passage towards the end of the last century; and it might have been expected that, since that time, some improvement should have taken place; but it is not so: the treatment of slaves by the British, subsequent to the Slave Regulation Act, and down to 1808, was mildness itself, when compared with the miseries consequent on the trade, and the system which has been pursued in the vain attempt to put it down, since that period to the present time. . . .

Since 1808 the English Government has, with various success, been indefatigably engaged in endeavouring to procure the co-operation of foreign powers for the suppression of the Slave Trade. In virtue of the treaties which have been entered into, many vessels engaged in the traffic have been captured; and much information has been obtained, which has been regularly laid before Parliament. A few of the cases which have been detailed will now be noticed, for the purpose of ascertaining whether the miseries which have been narrated have ceased to exist; or whether they do not *now* exist in a more intense degree than at any former period.

The first case I notice is that of the Spanish brig *Carlos*, captured in 1814. In this vessel of 200 tons, 512 negroes had been put on board (nearly 180 *more* than the complement allowed on the proportion of five slaves to three tons). The captor reported that

they were so miserably fed, clothed, &c., that any idea of the horrors of the Slave Trade would fall short of what I saw. Eighty were thrown overboard before we captured her. In many instances I saw the bones coming through the skin from starvation.

In the same year (1814) the schooner *Aglae*, of 40 tons, was captured with a cargo of 152 negroes (nearly four to each ton).

The only care seemed to have been to pack them as close as possible, and tarpaulin was placed over tarpaulin, in order to give the vessel the appearance of being laden with a well-stowed cargo of cotton and rice.

In 1815 a lieutenant of the navy thus describes the state of a Portuguese slaver, the *St. Joaquim:* he says,

*That within twenty-two days after the vessel had left Mozambique
thirteen of the slaves had died: that between the capture and their
arrival at Simon's Bay, the survivors of them were all sickly and weak,
and ninety-two of them afflicted with the flux; that the slaves were all
stowed together, perfectly naked, and nothing but rough, unplaned
planks to crouch down upon, in a hold situated over their water and
provisions, the place being little more than two feet in height, and the
space allowed for each slave so small, that it was impossible for them to
avoid touching and pressing upon those immediately surrounding. The
greater part of them were fastened, some three together, by one leg, each
in heavy iron shackles, a very large proportion of them having the flux.
Thus they were compelled,*

&c. (here a scene of disgusting wretchedness is described.)

*The pilot being asked by Captain Baker how many he supposed would
have reached their destination, replied, "About half the number that
were embarked."*

We have next the case of the *Rodeur*, as stated in a periodical work,
devoted to medical subjects, and published at Paris. This vessel, it appears,
was of 200 tons burden. She took on board a cargo of 160 negroes, and
after having been fifteen days on her voyage, it was remarked that the
slaves had contracted a considerable redness of the eyes, which spread
with singular rapidity. At this time they were limited to eight ounces of
water a-day for each person, which quantity was afterwards reduced to the
half of a wine-glass. By the advice of the surgeon, the slaves who were
in the hold were brought upon deck for the advantage of fresh air; but
it became necessary to abandon this expedient, as many of them who
were affected with nostalgia threw themselves into the sea, locked in each
other's arms. The ophthalmia, which had spread so rapidly and frightfully
among the Africans, soon began to infect all on board, and to create alarm
for the crew. The danger of infection, and perhaps the cause which produced the disease, were increased by a violent dysentery, attributed to the
use of rain-water. The number of the blind augmented every day. The
vessel reached Guadaloupe on June 21, 1819, her crew being in a most
deplorable condition. Three days after her arrival, the only man who during the voyage had withstood the influence of the contagion, and whom
Providence appeared to have preserved as a guide to his unfortunate com-
panions, was seized with the same malady. Of the negroes, thirty-nine
had become perfectly blind, twelve had lost one eye, and fourteen were
affected with blemishes more or less considerable.

This case excited great interest, and several additional circumstances connected with it were given to the public. It was stated that the captain caused several of the negroes who were prevented in the attempt to throw themselves overboard, to be shot and hung, in the hope that the example might deter the rest from a similar conduct. It is further stated, that upwards of thirty of the slaves who became blind were thrown into the sea and drowned; upon the principle that had they been landed at Guadaloupe, no one would have bought them, while by throwing them overboard the expense of maintaining them was avoided, and a ground was laid for a claim on the underwriters by whom the cargo had been insured, who are said to have allowed the claim, and made good the value of the slaves thus destroyed.

What more need be said in illustration of the extremity of suffering induced by the middle passage, as demonstrated by the case of the *Rodeur?* But the supplement must not be omitted. At the time when only one man could see to steer that vessel, a large ship approached,

> *which appeared to be totally at the mercy of the wind and the waves. The crew of this vessel, hearing the voices of the crew of the* Rodeur, *cried out most vehemently for help. They told the melancholy tale as they passed along,—that their ship was a Spanish slave-ship, the* St. Leon; *and that a contagion had seized the eyes of all on board, so that there was not one individual sailor or slave who could see. But alas! this pitiable narrative was in vain; for no help could be given. The* St. Leon *passed on, and was never more heard of!* . . .

I will endeavour to give a summary of the extent of the mortality incident to the middle passage. Newton states, that in his time it amounted to one-fourth, on the average, of the number embarked.

From papers presented to the House of Lords, in 1799, it appears that, in the year 1791, (three years after the passing of the Slave Carrying Regulation Act,) of 15,754 negroes embarked for the West Indies, &c., 1378 died during the passage, the average length of which was fifty-one days, showing a mortality of 8¾ per cent.

The amount of the mortality in 1792 was still greater. Of 31,554 slaves carried from Africa, no fewer than 5,413 died on the passage, making somewhat more than 17 per cent in fifty-one days.

Captain Owen, in a communication to the Admiralty, on the Slave Trade with the eastern coast of Africa, in 1823, states

That the ships which use this traffic consider they make an excellent voyage if they save one-third of the number embarked: some vessels are so fortunate as to save one-half of their cargo alive.

Captain Cook says, in the communication to which I have before alluded, as to the East coast traffic,

If they meet with bad weather, in rounding the Cape, their sufferings are beyond description; and in some instances one-half of the lives on board are sacrificed. In the case of the Napoleon, *from Quilimane, the loss amounted to two-thirds. It was stated to me by Captains and Supercargoes of other slavers, that they made a profitable voyage if they lost fifty per cent.; and that this was not uncommon.*

Caldcleugh says, "Scarcely two-thirds live to be landed."

Governor Maclean, of Cape Coast, who has had many opportunities of acquiring information on the subject, has stated to me, that he considers the average of deaths on the passage to amount to one-third.

Captain Ramsay, R.N., who was a long time on service with the Preventive Squadron, also stated to me, that the mortality on the passage across the Atlantic must be greater than the loss on the passage to Sierra Leone, from the greater liberty allowed after capture, and from the removal of the shackles. He believes the average loss to be one-third.

Rear-Admiral Sir Graham Eden Hamond, Commander-in-Chief on the South American station, in 1834, thus writes to the British Consul at Monte Video:

A slave-brig of 202 tons was brought into this port with 521 slaves on board. The vessel is said to have cleared from Monte Video in August last, under a licence to import 650 African colonists.

The licence to proceed to the coast of Africa is accompanied by a curious document, purporting to be an application from two Spaniards at Monte Video, named Villaca and Barquez, for permission to import 650 colonists, and 250 more — to cover the deaths on the voyage.

Here we have nearly one-third given apparently for the average loss on the passage, and this estimated by the slave-dealers themselves on the American side of the Atlantic.

Philip D. Curtin

A Historian's Recount

The horrors that abolitionists such as Buxton catalogued remain central to our understanding of the Middle Passage, but many modern historians have worked hard to define what was typical of a slaving voyage. Philip D. Curtin's immensely important 1969 study did much to start this trend by showing that the once accepted estimates of the size and destinations of the slave trade were of dubious accuracy. In the last part of this excerpt, this historian of Africa and the Atlantic summarizes his recalculation of the origins, destinations, and overall size of the slave trade.

This book . . . seeks to explore old knowledge, not to present new information. Its central aim is to bring together bits and pieces of incommensurate information already published, and to do this for only one aspect of the trade — the measurable number of people brought across the Atlantic. How many? When? From what parts of Africa? To what destinations in the New World? . . .

This book is . . . written with an implicit set of rules that are neither those of monographic research, nor yet those of a survey. Historical standards for monographic research require the author to examine every existing authority on the problem at hand, and every archival collection where part of the answer may be found. This has not been done. The rulebook followed here sets another standard. I have surveyed the literature on the slave trade, but not exhaustively. Where the authorities on some regional aspect of the trade have arrived at a consensus, and that consensus appears to be reasonable in the light of other evidence, I have let it stand. Where no consensus exists, or a gap occurs in a series of estimates, I have tried to construct new estimates. But these stop short of true research standards. I have not tried to go beyond the printed sources, nor into the relevant archives, even when they are known to contain important additional data. The task is conceived as that of

Philip D. Curtin, "A Historian's Recount," from *The Atlantic Slave Trade: A Census*, pp. xvi–xvii, 3–8, 165–173. Copyright © 1969. Reprinted by permission of the University of Wisconsin Press.

building with the bricks that exist, not in making new ones. This often requires the manipulation of existing data in search of commensurates. In doing this, I have tried to show the steps that lead from existing data to the new synthesis. Not everyone will agree with all the assumptions that go into the process, nor with all the forms of calculation that have been used. But this book is not intended to be a definitive study, only a point of departure that will be modified in time as new research produces new data, and harder data worthy of more sophisticated forms of calculation. It will have served its purpose if it challenges others to correct and complete its findings.

This point is of the greatest importance in interpreting any of the data that follow. One danger in stating numbers is to find them quoted later on with a degree of certitude that was never intended. This is particularly true when percentages are carried to tenths of 1 per cent, whereas in fact the hoped-for range of accuracy may be plus or minus 20 per cent of actuality. Let it be said at the outset, then, that most of the quantities that follow are wrong. They are not intended to be precise as given, only approximations where a result falling within 20 per cent of actuality is a "right" answer—that is, a successful result, given the quality of the underlying data. It should also be understood that some estimates will not even reach that standard of accuracy. They are given only as the most probable figures at the present state of knowledge. These considerations have made it convenient to round out most quantities to the nearest one hundred, including data taken from other authors.

All of this may seem to imply estimates of limited value on account of their limited accuracy. For many historical purposes, greater accuracy is not required, and some of the most significant implications of this quantitative study would follow from figures still less accurate than these. Their principal value is not, in any case, the absolute number, an abstraction nearly meaningless in isolation. It is, instead, the comparative values, making it possible to measure one branch of the slave trade against another.

Some readers may miss the sense of moral outrage traditional in histories of the trade. This book will have very little to say about the evils of the slave trade, still less in trying to assign retrospective blame to the individuals or groups who were responsible. This omission in no way implies that the slave trade was morally neutral; it clearly was not. The evils of the trade, however, can be taken for granted as a point long since proven beyond dispute. . . .

The principal secondary authorities and the principal textbooks are, indeed, in remarkable agreement on the general magnitude of the [Atlantic slave] trade. Most begin with the statement that little is known about the subject, pass on to the suggestion that it may be impossible to make an accurate numerical estimate, and then make an estimate. The style is exemplified by Basil Davidson's *Black Mother*, the best recent general history of the slave trade.

> *First of all, what were the round numbers involved in this forced emigration to which the African-European trade gave rise, beginning in the fifteenth century and ending in the nineteenth? The short answer is that nobody knows or ever will know: either the necessary records are missing or they were never made. The best one can do is to construct an estimate from confused and incomplete data.*

> *. . . For the grand total of slaves landed alive in the lands across the Atlantic an eminent student of population statistics, Kuczynski, came to the conclusion that fifteen millions might be "rather a conservative figure." Other writers have accepted this figure, though as a minimum: some have believed it was much higher than this.*

Roland Oliver and J. D. Fage in their *Short History of Africa*, the most widely-read history of Africa to appear so far, are less concerned to express their uncertainty, and they too come to a total estimate in the vicinity of fifteen million slaves landed. They go a step farther, however, and subdivide the total by centuries. . . .

The total is again given as a minimum, and it is clearly derived from R. R. Kuczynski. Indeed, Professor Fage gave the same breakdown in his *Introduction to the History of West Africa* and in his *Ghana*, where the citation of Kuczynski is explicit. The estimate is repeated by so many other recent authorities that it can be taken as the dominant statement of present-day historiography. Some writers cite Kuczynski directly. Others, like Robert Rotberg in his *Political History of Tropical Africa*, strengthen the case by citing both Kuczynski and a second author who derived his data from Kuczynski. Rotberg, however, improved on his authorities by raising the total to "at least twenty-five million slaves," an increase of two-thirds, apparently based on the general assurance that the fifteen-million figure was likely to be on the low side. Another alternative, chosen by D. B. Davis for his Pulitzer-Prize-winning *Problem of Slavery in Western Culture*, is not to bother with Kuczynski (who wrote, after all, more than thirty years ago), but to go directly to a recent authority—in this case to the words of Basil Davidson quoted above.

Since Kuczynski is at the center of this web of citations, quotations, and amplifications, it is important to see just how he went about calculating his now-famous estimates. The crucial passage in *Population Movements* does indeed present a general estimate of fifteen million or more slaves landed in the Americas, and it includes the distribution by centuries. . . . But Kuczynski himself shows no evidence of having made any calculation on his own. He merely found these estimates to be the most acceptable of those made by earlier authorities, and the particular authority he cited is none other than W. E. B. Du Bois.

Du Bois was, indeed, an eminent authority on Negro history, but Kuczynski's citation does *not* lead back to one of his works based on historical research. It leads instead to a paper on "The Negro Race in the United States of America," delivered to a semi-scholarly congress in London in 1911—a curious place to publish something as important as an original, overall estimate of the Atlantic slave trade—and in fact the paper contains no such thing. Du Bois's only mention of the subject in the place cited was these two sentences:

> The exact number of slaves imported is not known. Dunbar estimates that nearly 900,000 came to America in the sixteenth century, 2,750,000 in the seventeenth, 7,000,000 in the eighteenth, and over 4,000,000 in the nineteenth, perhaps 15,000,000 in all.

The real authority, then, is neither Kuczynski nor Du Bois, but Dunbar. Though Du Bois's offhand statement was not supported by footnotes or bibliography, the author in question was Edward E. Dunbar, an American publicist of the 1860s. During the early part of 1861, he was responsible for a serial called *The Mexican Papers*, devoted to furthering the cause of President Juárez of Mexico and of the Liberal Party in that country. The Liberals had just won the War of the Reform against their domestic opponents, but they were hard pressed by European creditors and threatened with possible military intervention—a threat that shortly materialized in the Maximilian affair. Dunbar's principal task was to enlist American sympathy, and if possible American diplomatic intervention, in support of Juárez' cause. But Dunbar was a liberal, by implication an anti-slavery man in American politics, and he published *The Mexican Papers* during the last months of America's drift into civil war. It was therefore natural that he should write an article called "History of the Rise and Decline of Commercial Slavery in America, with Reference to the Future of Mexico," and it was there that he published a set of estimates of the slave trade through time. . . . He remarked that these were only his own estimates, and he made the further reservation (so often repeated by his successors) that they were probably on the low side. . . .

The sequence is an impressive tower of authority, though it also suggests that even the best historians may be unduly credulous when they see a footnote to an illustrious predecessor. Basil Davidson should have identified the original author as "an obscure American publicist," rather than "an eminent student of population statistics," but the *ad hominem* fallacy is present in either case. Dunbar's obscurity is no evidence that he was wrong; nor does Kuczynski's use of Dunbar's estimates make them correct. The estimates were guesses, but they were guesses educated by a knowledge of the historical literature. They earned the approval of later generations who were in a position to be still better informed. Even though no one along the way made a careful effort to calculate the size of the trade from empirical evidence, the Dunbar estimates nevertheless represent a kind of consensus. . . .

It is now possible to look at the long-term movement of the Atlantic slave trade over a period of more than four centuries. The data make it abundantly clear that the eighteenth century was a kind of plateau in the history of the trade—the period when the trade reached its height, but also a period of slackening growth and beginning decline. The period 1741–1810 marks the summit of the plateau, when the long-term annual average rates of delivery hung just above 60,000 a year. The edge of the plateau was reached, however, just after the Peace of Utrecht in 1713, when the annual deliveries began regularly to exceed 40,000 a year, and the permanent drop below 40,000 a year did not come again until after the 1840s. Thus about 60 per cent of all slaves delivered to the New World were transported during the century 1721–1820. Eighty per cent of the total were landed during the century and a half, 1710–1850. . . .

It would be premature to generalize about the impact of the slave trade on African societies over these four centuries. On the other hand, historians have already begun to do so. The range of opinion runs the gamut from the view that the slave trade was responsible for virtually every unfavorable development in Africa over these centuries, to the opposite position that even the slave trade was better than no trade, that it was therefore a positive benefit to the African societies that participated. Since the results of this survey could be brought into the argument on either side, it is appropriate to enter a few caveats.

One conclusion that might be drawn is that, in reducing the estimated total export of slaves from about twenty million to about ten million, the harm done to African societies is also reduced by half. This is obvious nonsense. The demographic consequences of moving any number of people from any society can have meaning only in relation to the size of the society, the time-period concerned, the age and sex composition of the emigrants and of the society from which they depart. Until we know at least the size of the African population that supplied the slaves, the demographic implications of the ten-million estimate are just as indeterminate as those of the twenty-million estimate. As for the social or political consequences of the slave trade to African societies, these would not necessarily vary directly with the number exported. . . .

At best, the export data of the slave trade can be suggestive. If the dominant African pattern at the height of the slave trade was that of the militarized, slave-catching society, systematically preying on its neighbors, the export projections should show a relatively large and continuous supply of slaves from these hunter societies; and the slaves themselves should have been mainly from the less organized neighbors. This pattern does not emerge clearly from the slave-export data of eighteenth-century Africa. Some ports, notably the city-states of the Bight of Biafra, did produce a continuous supply that may imply slave-catching as an economic enterprise. Elsewhere, the rapid shift in sources of supply from one region to another suggests that by-product enslavement was the dominant feature, or that, if systematic slave-hunting were tried, it could not be maintained.

These weaknesses of quantitative evidence are important to keep in mind, if only because of a popular tendency to regard numbers as more "scientific" and reliable than other kinds of data. A great deal more could nevertheless be profitably done with the quantitative study of the slave trade. More and better samples of slave origins and better data on the numbers carried by the trade at particular times should make it possible to project the annual flow of slaves from particular societies, to take only one example. Even if the dimensions of the slave trade outlined here were as accurate as limited sources will ever allow—and they are not—still other dimensions of far greater significance for African and Atlantic history remain to be explored.

Herbert S. Klein

Profits and Losses

A professor of Latin American history at Columbia University, Herbert Klein summarizes a generation of research by scholars inspired by Curtin's statistical approach. Klein finds that the financial profits and the losses of human life associated with the slave trade, although substantial, were much smaller than the rough guesses of earlier historians. Like Curtin, he finds careful measurement a more useful tool than moral outrage in discovering the trade's secrets.

In recent decades there has been a fundamental change in the study of the Atlantic slave trade. From almost total neglect, the trade has become an area of major concern to economists and historians who have dedicated themselves to analyzing the African experience in America. Especially since the publication by Philip Curtin of his masterly synthesis *The Atlantic Slave Trade: A Census* in 1969, a massive amount of archival research has resulted in publications both of collections of documents from all the major archives of Europe, America, and Africa and of major works of synthesis on the demography, politics, and economics of the slave trade. . . .

From the work of the European economic historians, it is now evident that slave trade profits were not extraordinary by European standards. The average 10 percent rate obtained in studies of the eighteenth-century French and English slave traders was considered a good profit rate at the time but not out of the range of other contemporary investments. From a recent detailed study of the nineteenth century, it would seem that profits doubled in the next century largely as a result of rising slave prices in America, which in turn were due to the increasing suppression of the trade by the British navy. On average (except for some extraordinary voyages to Cuba in the 1850s), the rate of profit for nineteenth-century slavers was just under 20 percent. Thus, while profits in the special period of suppression in the nineteenth century were quite high, even these profits were not astronomic. . . .

Herbert S. Klein, "Profits and Losses," from "Economic Aspects of the Eighteenth-Century Atlantic Slave Trade" in *The Rise of the Merchant Empires*, ed. by James D. Tracy, 1990, pp. 287, 299, 303–308. Reprinted by permission of Cambridge University Press.

The conceptions prevalent in the popular literature about the relative costs of African slaves have their corollary hypotheses about the economics of their transportation. It was assumed that the low cost of the slaves made it profitable to pack in as many as the ship could hold without sinking and then accept high rates of mortality during the Atlantic crossing. If any slaves delivered alive were pure profit, then even the loss of several hundred would have made economic sense. But if the slaves were not a costless or cheap item to purchase, then the corresponding argument about "tight packing" also makes little sense. In fact, high losses on the crossing resulted in financial loss on the trip, as many ship accounts aptly prove.

Even more convincing than these theoretical arguments against reckless destruction of life is the fact that no study has yet shown a systematic correlation of any significance between the numbers of slaves carried and mortality at sea. Thousands of ship crossings have now been statistically analyzed, and none show a correlation of any significance between either tonnage or space available and mortality.

This does not mean that slaves were traveling in luxury. In fact, they had less room than did contemporary troops or convicts being transported. It simply means that after much experience and the exigencies of the trade, slavers only took on as many slaves as they could expect to cross the Atlantic safely. From scattered references in the pre-1700 period it seems that provisioning and carrying arrangements were initially deficient. But all post-1700 trade studies show that slavers carried water and provisions for double their expected voyage times and that in most trades they usually carried slightly fewer slaves than their legally permitted limits.

This increasing sophistication in the carrying of slaves was reflected in declining rates of mortality. In the pre-1700 trade, mean mortality rates over many voyages tended to hover around 20 percent. In turn this mean rate reflected quite wide variations, with many ships coming in with very low rates and an equally large number experiencing rates of double or more than double the mean figure. But in the post-1700 period the mean rates dropped, and the variation around the mean declined. By mid-century the mean stood at about 10 percent, and by the last quarter of the century all trades were averaging a rate of about 5 percent. Moreover the dispersion around these mean rates had declined, and two-thirds of the ships were experiencing no more than 5 percent variation above or below the mean rate.

These declines in mortality were due to the standardization increasingly adopted in the trade. First of all there developed a specialized and specifically constructed vessel used in the slave trade of most nations. By the second half of the eighteenth century slave ships were averaging two hundred tons among all European traders, a tonnage that seemed best to fit the successful carrying potential of the trade. Slave traders were also the first of the commercial traders to adopt copper sheathing for their ships, which was a costly new method to prolong the life of the vessels and guarantee greater speed. It should be stressed that these slave trade vessels were much smaller ships than Europeans used in either the West Indian or East Indian trades. This in turn goes a long way to explaining why the famous model of a triangular trade, long the staple of western textbooks, is largely a myth. This myth was based on the idea that the slave ships performed the multiple tasks of taking European goods to Africa, transporting slaves to America, and then bringing back the sugar or other slave-produced American staple for Europe all on the same voyage. In fact, the majority of American crops reached European markets in much larger and specially constructed West Indian vessels designed primarily for this shuttle trade; the majority of slavers returned to Europe with small cargoes or none at all; and in the largest slave trade of them all—that of Brazil—no slavers either departed from or returned to Europe.

All traders carried about two and a half slaves per ton, and although there was some variation in crew size and ratios, all slave trade ships carried at least twice the number of seamen needed to man the vessel, and thus double or more than that of any other long-distance oceanic trade. This very high ratio of sailors to tonnage was due to the security needs of controlling the slave prisoners. All the European slave traders were also using the same provisioning, health, and transportation procedures. They built temporary decks to house the slaves and divided them by age and sex. Almost all Europeans adopted smallpox vaccinations at about the same time, all carried large quantities of African provisions to feed the slaves, and all used the same methods for daily hygiene, care of the sick, and so on. This standardization explains the common experience of mortality decline, and it also goes a long way to rejecting contemporaneous assertions that any particular European trader was "better" or more efficient than any other.

Although these firmly grounded statistics on mortality certainly destroy many of the older beliefs about "astronomic" mortality and tight packing, there does remain the question of whether a 5 percent mortality rate for a thirty- to fifty-day voyage for a healthy young adult is high or low. If such a mortality rate had occurred among young adult peasants in eighteenth-century France, it would be considered an epidemic rate. Thus, although Europeans succeeded in reducing the rate to seemingly low percentages, these rates still represented extraordinary high death rate figures for such a specially selected population. Equally, although troop, immigrant, and convict mortality rates in the eighteenth century approached the slave death numbers, in the nineteenth century they consistently fell to below 1 percent for transatlantic voyages. For slaves, however, these rates never fell below 5 percent for any large group of vessels surveyed. There thus seems to have been a minimum death rate caused by the close quarters during transport, which the Europeans could never reduce.

Death in the crossing was due to a variety of causes. The biggest killers were gastrointestinal disorders, which were often related to the quality of food and water available on the trip, and fevers. Bouts of dysentery were common and the "bloody flux" as it was called could break out in epidemic proportions. The increasing exposure of the slaves to dysentery increased both the rates of contamination of supplies and the incidence of death. It was dysentery that accounted for the majority of deaths and was the most common disease experienced on all voyages. The astronomic rates of mortality reached on occasional voyages were due to outbreaks of smallpox, measles, or other highly communicable diseases that were not related to time at sea or the conditions of food and water supply, hygiene, and sanitation practices. It was this randomness of epidemic diseases that prevented even experienced and efficient captains from eliminating very high mortality rates on any given voyage.

Although time at sea was not usually correlated with mortality, there were some routes in which time was a factor. Simply because they were a third longer than any other routes, the East African slave trades that developed in the late eighteenth and nineteenth centuries were noted for overall higher mortality than the West African routes, even though mortality per day at sea was the same or lower than on the shorter routes. Also, just the transporting together of slaves from different epidemiological zones in Africa guaranteed the transmission of a host of local endemic diseases to all those who were aboard. In turn, this guaranteed the spread of all major African diseases to America.

Along with the impact of African diseases on the American populations, the biases in the age and sex of the migrating Africans also had a direct impact on the growth and decline of the American slave populations. The low ratio of women in each arriving ship, the fact that most of these slave women were mature adults who had already spent several of their fecund years in Africa, and the fact that few children were carried to America were of fundamental importance in the subsequent history of population growth. It meant that the African slaves who arrived in America could not reproduce themselves. The African women who did come to America had lost some potential reproductive years and were even less able to reproduce the total numbers of males and females in the original immigrant cohort, let alone create a generation greater than the total number who arrived from Africa. Even those American regions that experienced a heavy and constant stream of African slaves still had to rely on importation of more slaves to maintain their slave populations, let alone increase their size. Once that African migration stopped, however, it was possible for the slave populations to begin to increase through natural growth, so long as there was no heavy out-migration through emancipation.

It was this consistent negative growth of the first generation of African slaves which explains the growing intensity of the slave trade to America in the eighteenth and early nineteenth centuries. As the demand for American products grew in European markets because of the increasingly popular consumption of tobacco, cotton, coffee, and above all sugar, the need for workers increased and this could be met only by bringing in more Africans. It was only in the case of the United States that the growth of plantation crop exports to Europe did not lead to an increasing importation of African slaves. This was largely due to the very early North American experience of the local slave population achieving a positive growth rate and thus supplying its increasing labor needs from the positive growth of its native-born slave population. Although most demographic historians have shown that the Creole slave populations had positive growth rates from the beginning and that it was the distortions of the African-born cohorts that explain overall decline, more traditional historians have tried to explain the increasing demand for slaves as due to the low life expectancy of the Afro-American slave population. Much cited is the contemporary belief found in the planter literature of most colonies that the Afro-American slave experienced an average working life of "seven years." This myth of a short-lived labor force was related to the observed reality of slave population decline under the impact of heavy immigration of African slaves. Observers did not recognize the age and sexual imbalance of these Africans as a causal factor for the negative population growth of the slave labor force. Rather, they saw this decline as related to a very high mortality and low life expectancy. Yet all recent studies suggest both a positive rate of population growth among native-born slaves and a life expectancy well beyond the so-called average seven working years in all American societies.

The average life expectancy of slave males was in the upper twenties in Brazil, for example, and in the midthirties for the United States, which might suggest an average working life of at least twenty years in Brazil and twenty-five years in the United States. But this average figure, of course, takes into account the very high infant mortality rates. For those slaves who survived the first five years of life—and these are the only ones we are concerned with here—the comparable life expectancies was [*sic*] in the midthirties for the Brazilians and lower forties for the U.S. slaves. This suggests that the average working life was, at a minimum, twenty-five years for Brazilian slaves and thirty years for the U.S. ones—both figures far from the supposed seven-year average postulated in most histories.

David Eltis and David Richardson

The Achievements of the "Numbers Game"

Although Curtin was well aware that his recalculations were still flawed, his work inspired massive new research, provoked some heated controversies, and eventually led to the publication of more definitive tallies of the slave trade. David Eltis of Emory University and David Richardson of Hull University led a large international effort to compile a database, whose

David Eltis and David Richardson, "A New Assessment of the Transatlantic Slave Trade," in *Extending the Frontiers: Essays on the New Transatlantic Slave Trade Database*, 2008, p. 43. Copyright © 2008 Yale University Press. Reprinted by permission.

first public version included details of 27,233 slaving voyages and that has now grown to nearly 35,000. The new Transatlantic Slave Trade Database (TSTD2), available at www.slavevoyages.org, permits Internet users to analyze the African sources and New World destinations of the slave trade, both overall and year by year. This excerpt from their new guide is accompanied by charts from the database.

Philip Curtin's well-known 1969 book *The Atlantic Slave Trade: A Census* initiated the modern era of slave-trade studies and triggered a wave of research into slave-trading records in Europe, Africa, and the Americas. Almost forty years later, we are on the brink of a complete reconstruction of the history of the transatlantic slave trade from the early sixteenth century through to its close in 1867. The level of detail now possible was unimaginable when Curtin published his book. Where Curtin sought to track slaving activities by centuries or quarter centuries, we can now do so on an annual basis, at least from the mid-seventeenth century onward. Where Curtin grouped ship departures to Africa by nationality, and embarkations and disembarkations of slaves by African coastal regions or American colonies, we can now do the same on a port-by-port basis. Where Curtin could only identify places of embarkation and disembarkation of slaves separately, we can now reveal links across the Atlantic and track how they changed through time. Where Curtin could only measure shipboard mortality through the percentage of losses of slaves in transit, we can now estimate shipboard mortality rates and the factors that helped to shape them. The evidential base for the study of the Atlantic slave trade (and the computational capacity for storing and interrogating it) has been revolutionized. . . .

In assessing the size of the trade, Curtin had to choose between totals taken from the African side (using shipping records) and totals from the American side (using a combination of shipping and demographic data). He chose the latter and then projected what the departures from Africa must have been if mortality had averaged 15 percent of those taken on board. On this basis, he estimated just under 9.6 million arrivals in the Americas and then about 11.25 million departures from Africa. Curiously, the debate and extensive research activity that Curtin's book triggered concentrated primarily on his total estimates, rather than on the implicit challenge he had thrown down to scholars to reconcile the differences between his arrivals and departures estimates.

One of the main contributions of recent research on shipping data, both transatlantic and intra-American, has been to eliminate these discrepancies between African departures and American arrivals. First, more detailed information on individual voyages has shown significant losses of ships before they embarked slaves at the African coast. Such losses stemmed from natural hazard and from the actions of Africans, privateers, pirates, and European rivals. Second, much more is now known about the forced movement of slaves after their arrival in the Americas. The largest intra-American movement of slaves before the nineteenth century was in Brazil and was by land, but in the Caribbean the British organized a large water-borne traffic that also redistributed slaves from the British to the Spanish and French Americas. Thanks to the new data in TSTD2, discrepancies in shipping data between departures and arrivals no longer exist. Scholars may now use migration estimates derived from demographic data as an independent check on the voyage-based data, rather than as method for filling in gaps in the shipping records—at least after 1700.

A summary of our assessment of the completeness of the current database is presented in Figure [1], which lays out a crude time profile of the transatlantic slave trade over three and a half centuries. The top function in Figure [1] is taken from the new estimates . . . , grouped in twenty-five-year . . . intervals. The lower function, by contrast, is based on the data taken directly from TSTD2. The difference between the two functions represents our present assessment of the voyages that occurred but which have not left a record. . . .

. . . Portuguese vessels are now thought to have accounted for 46.5 percent of the traffic, and the British around 26 percent. The difference between the two is largely explained by the late arrival of the British into the trade and their early departure with the 1807 abolition act. As long as they continued in the business, they dominated the northern wind and current system almost as much as the Portuguese dominated the traffic south of the equator. Of the others, the Spanish pattern of involvement was the inverse of that of the British. After major involvement with the Portuguese prior to the separation of the Iberian crowns in 1640, the Spanish carried almost no slaves in the eighteenth century prior to the last decade. They then reentered the traffic to the point where they came to dominate the northern wind and current routes as effectively as the British had in the previous century. For the French, the major determinant of participation was war. From 1689 to 1831, the French

FIGURE 1.   Slaves Leaving Africa by Quarter Century:
              Estimated, Compared to Recorded in TSTD2.

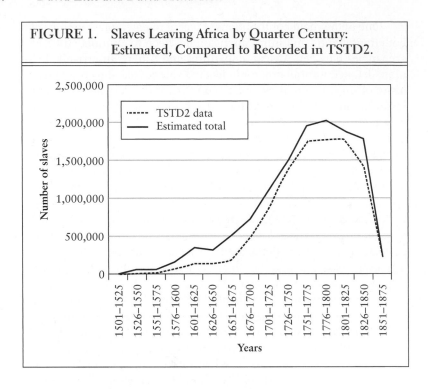

flag frequently disappeared altogether during hostilities. This apart, the trajectory of their trade was similar to the British, except that it continued for a further quarter century after British withdrawal. The Dutch, by contrast, were most important in the seventeenth century and carried few slaves after the British destroyed a good part of their merchant marine between 1780 and 1784. . . .

How do the new totals compare with the 2001 attempt to provide an overall assessment of the slave trade's size? As already noted, in 2001 one of us estimated total slave departures from Africa at 11.062 million. We now think that 12.521 million were carried off—an increase of 13 percent. At the time of this writing, aggregate arrivals in the Americas are thought to have been 10.703 million, an 11 percent increase over 2001's estimate of 9.657 million. On the African side, the infusion of new material has not changed the regional distribution by much. Upper Guinea and the Gold Coast are now seen to have been slightly more important relative to the rest of Africa, and the Bights of Benin and Biafra slightly less. West Central and Southeast Africa, by contrast, remain in the same relative positions. On the American side of the Atlantic, the relative distribution has shifted toward Bahia [in northeast Brazil] and away from the British Caribbean, especially Jamaica, with most of the other major regions keeping the shares that they held in 2001. The new data [see Figure 2] thus have not threatened the dominance of West Central Africa and Brazil, but this is hardly surprising. The major benefit of the new information has been to increase our understanding of the links between Africa and the Americas and, of course, to provide much more detail about those links. Space constraints mean that a fuller explication of this facet of the trade must be reserved for a different occasion. Our major hope is that the revised data set will be used for purposes far beyond estimating the size of the slave trade.

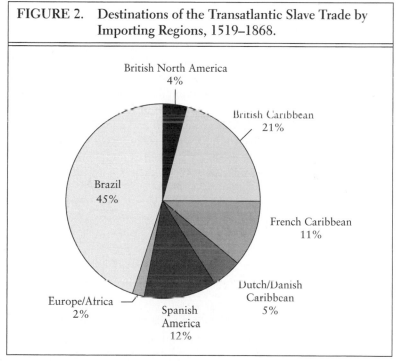

FIGURE 2. Destinations of the Transatlantic Slave Trade by Importing Regions, 1519–1868.

British North America 4%

British Caribbean 21%

Brazil 45%

French Caribbean 11%

Dutch/Danish Caribbean 5%

Spanish America 12%

Europe/Africa 2%

Source: Transatlantic Slave Trade Database, www.slavevoyages.org.

Most debates over issues of agency, identity, cultural patterns, gender, and resistance would not exist without an often implicit quantitative component. . . .

With the appearance of a renewable voyage-based data source, and the major infusion of younger blood as represented in the present essays, we hope that a new era of engagement, debate, and critical evaluation is about to begin. But the issues of this new work will no doubt differ from past concerns. It may seem that the major thrust of the research presented here is to add weight to Curtin's critics. This is, of course, a central part of the present volume, although we expect that the . . . estimates of close to or in excess of 13 million transported slaves are too high to find support in voyage-based evidence. The main contribution of the new work in quantitative issues should be viewed as reconciling the discrepancies to which Curtin pointed between the estimates of arrivals in the Americas and estimates of departures from Africa—an issue that few of Curtin's critics engaged. For the first time in forty years, it is possible to see a broad picture that offers mutually reinforcing data on both sides of the Atlantic. We argue that there is a now a high degree of internal consistency and reliability about the aggregate estimates of the slave trade. More important, we would like to think that TSTD2 will shift attention away from the overall assessment of the slave trade and toward a tighter focus on individual branches of the slave trade and the thousands of ports that were involved in the business. Researchers now have the means with which to both draw on and add details to voyages for all branches of the slave trade. In the process, they will find it possible to address issues of far greater import than merely the size of the slave trade. Perhaps this book will be the last to devote a major part of its thrust to assessing the overall size of the slave trade.

PART

 Effects in Africa

——————— VARIETY OF OPINION ———————

With the help of the king ... [we] assaulted the town ... [and] took 250 persons.

JOHN HAWKINS, 1568

The truth is that a developing Africa went into slave trading and European commercial relations as into a gale-force wind, which shipwrecked a few societies, set many others off course, and generally slowed down the rate of advance.

WALTER RODNEY

The coastal exports of young adult slaves, twice as many men as women, tended to transform the structure of the population and the organization of society.

PATRICK MANNING

European trade with Africa can scarcely be seen as disruptive in itself, for it did not oust any line of African production, nor did it thwart development.

JOHN THORNTON

87

John Hawkins

An Alliance to Raid for Slaves

Because it is mentioned in two of the modern selections that follow, it is useful to begin with an early account of the slave trade by John Hawkins (1532–1595). Backed by powerful investors, this ambitious privateer from Plymouth, England, made three profitable slaving voyages to Guinea (as West Africa was then called) in the 1560s. This excerpt from his third voyage shows how trading and raiding were closely associated in the early English slave trade, but it also suggests how closely the European's success depended on finding an African ally who would cooperate with him—up to a point.

The ships departed from Plymouth, the second day of October, Anno 1567 and . . . arrived at Cape Verde, the eighteenth of November: where we landed 150 men, hoping to obtain some Negroes, where we got but few, and those with great hurt and damage to our men, which chiefly proceeded of their envenomed arrows: and although in the beginning they seemed to be but small hurts, yet there hardly escaped any that had blood drawn of them, but died in strange sort, with their mouths shut some ten days before they died, and after their wounds were whole; where I myself had one of the greatest wounds, yet thanks be to God, escaped. From thence we passed the time upon the coast of Guinea, unto Sierra Leone, till the twelfth of January, in which time we had not gotten together a hundred and fifty Negroes: yet notwithstanding the sickness of our men, and the late time of the year commanded us away; and thus having nothing wherewith to seek the coast of the West Indies, I was with the rest of the company in consultation to go to the coast of the Mine [i.e., the Gold Coast], hoping there to have obtained some gold for our wares, and thereby to have defrayed our charge. But even in that present instant, there came to us a Negro, sent from

From "The Third Troublesome Voyage . . . to the Parts of Guinea, and the West Indies, in the Yeeres 1567 and 1568 by M. John Hawkins," in Richard Hakluyt, *The Principal Navigations, Voyages, Traffiques and Discoveries of the English Nation* (New York, 1928) pp. 53–55. Spelling has been modernized.

a king, oppressed by other kings, his neighbors, desiring our aid, with [the] promise that as many Negroes as by these wars might be obtained, as well of his part as of ours, should be at our pleasure; whereupon we concluded to give aid, and sent 120 of our men, which the 15 of January, assaulted a town of the Negroes of our ally's adversaries, which had in it 8,000 inhabitants, being very strongly impaled and fenced after their manner, but it was so well defended, that our men prevailed not, but lost six men and forty hurt: so that our men sent forthwith to me for more help: whereupon considering the good success of this enterprise might highly further the commodity of our voyage, I went myself, and with the help of the king of our side, assaulted the town, both by land and sea, and very hardly with fire (their houses being covered with dry palm leaves) obtained the town, put the inhabitants to flight, where we took 250 persons, men, women, & children, and by our friend the king of our side, there were taken 600 prisoners, whereof we hoped to have our choice: but the Negro (in whose nation is seldom or never found truth) meant nothing less: for that night he removed his camp and prisoners, so that we were fain to content us with those few which we had gotten ourselves.

Walter Rodney

The Unequal Partnership Between Africans and Europeans

During the next three hundred years, the Atlantic slave trade changed in many ways. As the late West Indian historian Walter Rodney notes, Europeans obtained slaves by trading rather than raiding. But in this excerpt, published in 1972, Rodney also argues that the balance of power in the trading relationship soon shifted in favor of the European partners. The trade caused Africa to suffer population loss, deflected African energy away from productive activities, undercut African manufacturing with cheap manufactured goods, and tied Africans into an inferior relationship with a European capitalist economy that stifled their economic and technological progress. Although Rodney notes that many parts of Africa progressed during the era of the slave trade, he insists that these advances were despite the Atlantic trade, not because of it.

. . . Undoubtedly, with few exceptions such as Hawkins, European buyers purchased African captives on the coasts of Africa and the transaction between themselves and Africans was a form of trade. It is also true that very often a captive was sold and resold as he made his way from the interior to the port of embarkation—and that too was a form of trade. However, on the whole, the process by which captives were obtained on African soil was not trade at all. It was through warfare, trickery, banditry, and kidnaping. When one tries to measure the effect of European slave trading on the African continent, it is essential to realize that one is measuring the effect of social violence rather than trade in any normal sense of the word.

Many things remain uncertain about the slave trade and its consequences for Africa, but the general picture of destructiveness is clear, and that destructiveness can be shown to be the logical consequence of the manner of recruitment of captives in Africa. . . .

African economic activity was affected both directly and indirectly by population loss. For instance, when the inhabitants of a given area were reduced below a certain number in an environment where the tsetse fly was present, the remaining few had to abandon the area. In effect, enslavement was causing these people to lose their battle to tame and harness nature—a battle which is at the basis of development. Violence almost meant insecurity. The opportunity presented by European slave dealers became the major (though not the only) stimulus for a great deal of social violence between different African communities and within any given community. It took the form more of raiding and kidnaping than of regular warfare, and that fact increased the element of fear and uncertainty.

Both openly and by implication, all the European powers in the nineteenth century indicated their awareness of the fact that the activities connected with producing captives were inconsistent with other economic pursuits. That was the time when Britain in particular wanted Africans to collect palm produce and rubber and to grow agricultural crops for export in place of slaves; and it was clear that slave raiding was violently conflicting with that objective in Western, Eastern, and Central Africa. Long before that date, Europeans accepted that fact when their self-interest was involved. For example, in the seventeenth century, the Portuguese and Dutch actually discouraged slave trade on the Gold Coast, for they recognized that it would be incompatible with gold trade. However, by the end of that century, gold had been discovered in Brazil, and the importance of gold supplies from Africa was lessened. Within the total Atlantic pattern, African slaves became more important than gold, and Brazilian gold was offered for African captives at Whydah (Dahomey) and Accra. At that point, slaving began undermining the Gold Coast economy and destroying the gold trade. Slave raiding and kidnaping made it unsafe to mine and to travel with gold; and raiding for captives proved more profitable than gold mining. One European on the scene noted that "as one fortunate marauding makes a native rich in a day, they therefore exert themselves rather in war, robbery and plunder than in their old business of digging and collecting gold."

The above changeover from gold mining to slave raiding took place within a period of a few years between 1700 and 1710, when the Gold Coast came to supply about five thousand to six thousand captives per year. By the end of the eighteenth century, a much smaller number of captives were exported from the Gold Coast, but the damage had already been done. It is worth noting that Europeans sought out different parts of West and Central Africa at different times to play the role of major suppliers of slaves to the Americas. This meant that virtually every section of the long western coastline between the Senegal and Cunene rivers had at least a few years' experience of intensive trade in slaves—with all its consequences. Besides, in the history of eastern Nigeria, the Congo, northern Angola, and Dahomey, there were periods extending over decades when exports remained at an average of many thousands per year. Most of those areas were also relatively highly developed within the African context. They were leading forces inside Africa, whose energies would otherwise have gone towards their own self-improvement and the betterment of the continent as a whole.

The changeover to warlike activities and kidnapping must have affected all branches of economic activity, and agriculture in particular. Occasionally, in certain localities food production was increased to provide supplies for slave ships, but the overall consequences of slaving on agricultural activities in Western, Eastern, and Central Africa were negative. Labor was drawn off from agriculture and conditions became unsettled. Dahomey, which in the sixteenth century was known for exporting food to parts of what is now Togo, was suffering from famines in the nineteenth century. The present generation of Africans will readily recall that in the colonial period when able-bodied men left their homes as migrant laborers, that upset the farming routine in the home districts and often caused famines. Slave trading after all meant migration of labor in a manner one hundred times more brutal and disruptive.

To achieve economic development, one essential condition is to make the maximum use of the country's labor and natural resources. Usually, that demands peaceful conditions, but there have been times in history when social groups have grown stronger by raiding their neighbors for women, cattle, and goods, because they then used the "booty" from the raids for the benefit of their own community. Slaving in Africa did not even have that redeeming value. Captives were shipped outside instead of being utilized within any given African community for creating wealth from nature. It was only as an accidental by-product that in some areas Africans who recruited captives for Europeans realized that they were better off keeping some captives for themselves. In any case, slaving prevented the remaining population from effectively engaging in agriculture and industry, and it employed professional slave-hunters and warriors to destroy rather than build. Quite apart from the moral aspect and the immense suffering that it caused, the European slave trade was economically totally irrational from the viewpoint of African development. . . .

One tactic that is now being employed by certain European (including American) scholars is to say that the European slave trade was undoubtedly *a moral evil*, but it was *economically good* for Africa. Here attention will be drawn only very briefly to a few of those arguments to indicate how ridiculous they can be. One that receives much emphasis is that African rulers and other persons obtained European commodities in exchange for their captives, and this was how Africans gained "wealth." This suggestion fails to take into account the fact that several European imports were competing with and strangling African products; it fails to take into account the fact that none of the long list of European articles were of the type which entered into the productive process, but were rather items to be rapidly consumed or stowed away uselessly; and it incredibly overlooks the fact that the majority of the imports were of the worst quality even as consumer goods—cheap gin, cheap gun powder, pots and kettles full of holes, beads, and other assorted rubbish.

Following from the above, it is suggested that certain African kingdoms grew strong economically and politically as a consequence of the trade with Europeans. The greatest of the West African kingdoms, such as Oyo, Benin, Dahomey, and Asante, are cited as examples. Oyo and Benin were great long before making contact with Europeans, and while both Dahomey and Asante grew stronger during the period of the European slave trade, the roots of their achievements went back to much earlier years. Furthermore—and this is a major fallacy in the argument of the slave trade apologists—the fact that a given African state grew politically more powerful at the same time as it engaged in selling captives to Europeans is not automatically to be attributed to the credit of the trade in slaves. A cholera epidemic may kill thousands in a country and yet the population increases. The increase obviously came about *in spite of* and not because of the cholera. This simple logic escapes those who speak about the European slave trade benefiting Africa. The destructive tendency of slave trading can be clearly established; and, wherever a state seemingly progressed in the epoch of slave trading, the conclusion is simply that it did so in spite of the adverse effects of a process that was more damaging than cholera. This is the picture that emerges from a detailed study of Dahomey, for instance, and in the final analysis although Dahomey did its best to expand politically and militarily while still tied to slave trade, that form of economic activity seriously undermined its economic base and left it much worse off.

A few of the arguments about the economic benefits of the European slave trade for Africa amount to nothing more than saying that exporting millions of captives was a way of avoiding starvation in Africa! To attempt to reply to that would be painful and time-wasting. But, perhaps a slightly more subtle version of the same argument requires a reply: namely, the argument that Africa gained because in the process of slave trading new food crops were acquired from the American continent and these became staples in Africa. The crops in question are maize and cassava, which became staples in Africa late in the nineteenth century and in the present century. But the spread of food crops is one of the most common phenomena in human history. . . .

All of the above points are taken from books and articles published recently, as the fruit of research in major British and American universities. They are probably not the commonest views even among European bourgeois scholars, but they are representative of a growing trend that seems likely to become the new accepted orthodoxy in metropolitan capitalist countries; and this significantly coincides with Europe's struggle against the further decolonization of Africa economically and mentally. In one sense, it is preferable to ignore such rubbish and isolate our youth from its insults; but unfortunately one of the aspects of current African underdevelopment is that the capitalist publishers and bourgeois scholars dominate the scene and help mold opinions the world over. It is for that reason that writing of the type which justifies the trade in slaves has to be exposed as racist bourgeois propaganda, having no connection with reality or logic. It is a question not merely of history but of present-day liberation struggle in Africa.

It has already been indicated that in the fifteenth century European technology was not totally superior to that of other parts of the world. There were certain features which were highly advantageous to Europe—such as shipping and (to a lesser extent) guns. Europeans trading to Africa had to make use of Asian and African consumer goods, showing that their system of production was not absolutely superior. It is particularly striking that in the early centuries of trade, Europeans relied heavily on Indian cloths for resale in Africa, and they also purchased cloths on several parts of the West African coast for resale elsewhere. Morocco, Mauritania, Senegambia, Ivory Coast, Benin, Yorubaland, and Loango were all exporters to other parts of Africa—through European middlemen. . . .

African demand for cloth was increasing rapidly in the fifteenth, sixteenth, and seventeenth centuries, so that there was a market for all cloth produced locally as well as room for imports from Europe and Asia. But, directed by an acquisitive capitalist class, European industry increased its capacity to produce on a large scale by harnessing the energy of wind, water, and coal. European cloth industry was able to copy fashionable Indian and African patterns, and eventually to replace them. Partly by establishing a stranglehold on the distribution of cloth around the shores of Africa, and partly by swamping African products by importing cloth in bulk, European traders eventually succeeded in putting an end to the expansion of African cloth manufacture.

. . . When European cloth became dominant on the African market, it meant that African producers were cut off from the increasing demand. The craft producers either abandoned their tasks in the face of cheap available European cloth, or they continued on the same small hand-worked instruments to create styles and pieces for localized markets. Therefore, there was what can be called "technological arrest" or stagnation, and in some instances actual regression, since people forgot even the simple techniques of their forefathers. The abandonment of traditional iron smelting in most parts of Africa is probably the most important instance of technological regression.

Development means a capacity for self-sustaining growth. It means that an economy must register advances which in turn will promote further progress. The loss of industry and skill in Africa was extremely small, if we measure it from the viewpoint of modern scientific achievements or even by standards of England in the late eighteenth century. However, it must be borne in mind that to be held back at one stage means that it is impossible to go on to a further stage. When a person was forced to leave school after only two years of primary school education, it is no reflection on him that he is academically and intellectually less developed than someone who had the opportunity to be schooled right through to university level. What Africa experienced in the early centuries of trade was precisely a loss of development *opportunity*, and this is of the greatest importance. . . .

The European slave trade was a direct block, in removing millions of youth and young adults who are the human agents from whom inventiveness springs. Those who remained in areas badly hit by slave capturing were preoccupied about their freedom rather than with improvements in production. Besides, even the busiest African in West, Central, or East Africa was concerned more with trade than with production, because of the nature of the contacts with Europe; and that situation was not conducive to the introduction of technological advances. The most dynamic groups over a great area of Africa became associated with foreign trade — notably, the Afro-Portuguese middlemen of Upper Guinea, the Akan market women, the Aro traders of Mozambique, and the Swahili and Wanyamwezi of East Africa. The trade which they carried on was in export items like captives and ivory which did not require the invention of machinery. Apart from that, they were agents for distributing European imports. . . .

Apart from inventiveness, we must also consider the borrowing of technology. When a society for whatever reason finds itself technologically trailing behind others, it catches up not so much by independent inventions but by borrowing. Indeed, very few of man's major scientific discoveries have been separately discovered in different places by different people. Once a principle or a tool is known, it spreads or diffuses to other peoples. Why then did European technology fail to make its way into Africa during the many centuries of contact between the two continents? The basic reason is that the very nature of Afro-European trade was highly unfavorable to the movement of positive ideas and techniques from the European capitalist system to the African pre-capitalist (communal, feudal, and prefeudal) system of production. . . . Placing the whole question in historical perspective allows us to see that capitalism has always discouraged technological evolution in Africa, and blocks Africa's access to its own technology. . . . [C]apitalism introduced into Africa only such limited aspects of its material culture as were essential to more efficient exploitation, but the general tendency has been for capitalism to underdevelop Africa in technology.

The European slave trade and overseas trade in general had what are known as "multiplier effects" on Europe's development in a very positive sense. This means that the benefits of foreign contacts extended to many areas of European life not directly connected with foreign trade, and the whole society was better equipped for its own internal development. The opposite was true of Africa not only in the crucial sphere of technology but also with regard to the size and purpose of each economy in Africa. Under the normal processes of evolution, an economy grows steadily larger so that after a while two neighboring economies merge into one. That was precisely how national economies were created in the states of Western Europe through the gradual combination of what were once separate provincial economies. Trade with Africa actually helped Europe to weld together more closely the different national economies, but in Africa there was disruption and disintegration at the local level. At the same time, each local economy ceased to be directed exclusively or even primarily towards the satisfaction of the wants of its inhabitants; and (whether or not the particular Africans recognized it) their economic effort served external interests and made them dependent on those external forces based in Western Europe. In this way, the African economy taken as a whole was diverted away from its previous line of development and became distorted.

Patrick Manning

Social and Demographic Transformations

Historian Patrick Manning of the University of Pittsburg places his interpretation of the slave trade's impact in the context of schools of historical interpretation that go back more than two centuries. He contrasts older views of African societies as static with modern historians' presumption of an "African dynamism" and further distinguishes between those who see Africa's history as controlled from within ("emergent Africa") and those who see it as externally dominated ("Afrique engagée"). He places Rodney in the latter school, but he criticizes Rodney's view that Africa was simultaneously being stifled by its relationship with capitalism while some parts of the continent were experiencing positive development despite the trade. In effect, Manning faults Rodney for trying to have one foot in each camp. Manning then goes on to support the interpretation of "Afrique engagée," stressing that the demographic and social effects of the slave trade were interconnected with the economic effects, a point that he subsequently developed in his book *Slavery and African Life: Occidental, Oriental and African Slave Trades* (1990).

The old interpretations and the old disputes on Africa and the slave trade have left their mark. The vision of eternal Africa allowed room for disagreement about the impact of the slave trade, and these disagreements have found their way into the current literature. The contrasting interpretations separated those who contended that the transatlantic commerce in slaves brought major changes to African societies from those who denied that trade in slaves disturbed the African social order. Archibald Dalzel, the eighteenth-century English slave trader and propagandist, argued that African society remained unaffected, and he quoted King

Patrick Manning, "Social and Demographic Transformations" from "Contours of Slavery and Social Change in Africa," *American Historical Review* vol. 88 no. 4 October 1983, pp. 836–839, 844–851, 853, 856–857. Copyright © 1983. Reprinted by permission of the author.

Kpengla of Danhomè* in support of his position. David Livingstone, the mid-nineteenth-century explorer and missionary, argued forcefully that, to the contrary, slavery and the slave trade were devastating to African society. At the turn of the twentieth century Sir Harry Hamilton Johnston, an imperial man-on-the-spot and amateur scholar, attempted to synthesize these conflicting positions in an interpretation that is in some ways more optimistic than either: "Abominable as the slave trade has been in filling Tropical Africa with incessant warfare and rapine . . . , its ravages will soon be repaired by a few decades of peace and security during which this prolific, unextinguishable negro race will rapidly increase its numbers."

Both the similarities and the differences among these arguments are instructive. Dalzel and Johnston saw African societies as robust and able to withstand the pressures of the slave trade, while Livingstone viewed African societies as fragile and easily shattered. All three, however, shared the view of African societies as static. Although it had survived the slave trade intact, the "prolific, unextinguishable negro race," in Johnston's words, had not progressed—had not gained the ability "to start the children from a higher level than the parents." This vision of eternal Africa, emphasizing stagnation and resistance to change, took root and survived in the minds of observers largely because of the difficulty of knowing what changes had taken place. This difficulty, in turn, stemmed not only from the scarcity and dispersal of documentation on precolonial Africa but also from the blurring of perception brought about by cultural differences between African and European observers.

Contemporary Africanist historians have shown remarkable success in bridging the gaps within the documentary record and between cultures, not least because of the growing number of African contributors to the literature. Yet the rise of the Africanist tradition has not been sufficient to resolve the role of the slave trade in precolonial Africa. Instead, the earlier contending views—whether trade in slaves exerted great or small influence on African historical development—have aligned themselves with two interpretive tendencies that have grown up within the Africanist literature. For instance, Basil Davidson, writing in the early 1960s when many African countries were regaining their independence, argued, "Viewed as a factor in African history, the precolonial connection with Europe—essentially, the slave trade—had

---

*Also spelled "Dahomey." *Ed.*

powerfully degrading consequences for the structure of society." Some years later John D. Fage brought to the debate the revised figures on the magnitude of the slave trade; he concluded that the eighteenth-century loss of four million persons from West Africa did not reduce its population, and he later added that the region's social institutions similarly remained unaffected. Considering many of the same data but also taking underdevelopment into account, Walter Rodney reasoned that, on the contrary, the trade in slaves had brought great harm to African economic and political structures. A decade later Joseph C. Miller argued, with reference to West Central Africa, that a domestically generated cycle of drought, disease, and famine did more to limit population and provoke social change than did the impact of slave exports.

All of the participants in this recent discussion of the impact of the slave trade on Africa have assumed an African dynamism. The differences among them are in the relative emphases they have given to external forces of change. Can the external forces be safely minimized and treated as boundary conditions for a situation in which the major forces for change were domestic, as Fage and Miller have argued? Such an analytical approach may be termed the vision of "emergent Africa": as the historical reconstruction of African social change has become increasingly detailed, this approach has become widely influential in the thinking of Africanist historians. Or must external factors be drawn fully into the analysis of precolonial forces for change, as Davidson and Rodney have contended? This is the vision of "Afrique engagée," which focuses on such interactions as much as on domestic evolution. The choice between the two is determined by ascertaining which leads to the most detailed and yet elegant interpretation of the historical record.

John Fage's view of the role of the slave trade in precolonial Africa dominated the opinions of historians during the 1970s. For West Africa, Fage compared eighteenth-century slave exports that averaged forty thousand per year with a population he estimated at twenty-five million and a growth rate he estimated at 1.5 per thousand—or, some thirty-eight thousand—per year. Hence, "the effect of the export slave trade in the eighteenth century may have been more or less to check population growth," and its impact was in consequence minimal even at the height of slave exports. Fage continued, "The conclusion to which one is led, therefore, is that whereas in East and Central Africa the slave trade, sometimes conducted in the interior by raiding and warring strangers, could be extremely destructive of economic, political and social life, in

West Africa it was part of a sustained process of economic and political development." West Africa's domestic processes of evolution were potent enough, in Fage's view, to absorb, neutralize, and, conceivably, even benefit from the effects of participation in slave exports. Although he admitted that the negative effects of slave trade might have been greater outside of West Africa, other scholars have claimed that, particularly for Central Africa, the population and social institutions successfully withstood the pressures of the slave trade. This is the vision of emergent Africa, as applied to the impact of the trade in slaves.

Basil Davidson and Walter Rodney, while basing their views on the assumption of an evolving, developing African society, nevertheless asserted that the slave trade had a significantly detrimental effect on African society. Theirs was a vision of a precolonial Afrique engagée and of a continent that suffered from the engagement. The details of their arguments, however, rely not so much on demographic reasoning (both assumed that the African population did not decline) as on the interruption of African institutional and social progress. "The years of trial," as Davidson called the precolonial era, "were years of isolation and paralysis wherever the trade with Europe, essentially a trade in slaves, could plant its sterilizing hand." Although Davidson, with his slaves-for-guns thesis, and Rodney, with his underdevelopment thesis, listed striking examples to support this view, neither was able to develop a sustained and detailed analysis. Moreover, their image of the meeting of European and African influences depicted not so much a true interaction of the two as the truncation of the latter by the former. Their interpretation thus veers back toward Harry Johnston's image of eternal Africa, except that Davidson and Rodney emphasized the negative, rather than the positive, contributions of European contact to African development.

With a reformulation of the argument, however, the vision of Afrique engagée has gained validity as the relevant framework for interpreting the role of the slave trade in precolonial African history. The limits of Fage's interpretation are centered in his aggregative approach: he did not give much attention to the breakdown of slave exports by sex or age or to the impact of changes in quantities and prices of slave exports over time. Disaggregation of the data, when combined with analysis based on demographic principles and price theory, leads to results that are different from, and in some cases contradictory to, those previously accepted. The interactions of the New World demand for slaves with domestic conditions in Africa brought about—long before the late nineteenth century Scramble for Africa—pervasive social change. Such social changes included the expansion and subsequent transformation of polygyny, the development of two different types of African slavery, the creation and subsequent impoverishment of a class of African merchants, and a final expansion of slavery in the decades before the Scramble. Although the most profound changes from the interaction of the slave trade and African conditions occurred along the western coast of Africa, almost all regions of Africa were touched by the influence of the export trade at one time or another. . . .

The Atlantic slave trade before 1650 rarely carried more than ten thousand slaves per year. Its aggregate impact on the continent was, therefore, small, although the experiences of certain regions prefigured the sharp pressures that were subsequently felt on a broader scale. The Kongo kingdom, for instance, became the main source of slaves for the sugar plantations of São Thomé in the sixteenth century, and numerous sources confirm the corrosive effect of slave exports on Kongo political structure and on the spread of Christianity there. The Upper Guinea Coast supplied large numbers of slaves (predominantly male) as New World laborers in the early seventeenth century, and accounts of contemporary observers give strong support to the image of a predominantly female society left behind, in which women took over agricultural and fishing tasks to assure sufficient production. Although only these two regions, Senegambia, and perhaps the kingdom of Benin exported enough slaves in these early days to influence population size and composition, virtually every region on the western coast of Africa provided some slaves to European purchasers in the years before 1650. But slaves had not yet become Africa's dominant export: gold exports, especially from the Gold Coast, exceeded the value of African slave exports until the end of the seventeenth century.

A qualitative change in the slave trade took form at the turn of the eighteenth century; a four-fold increase in slave prices occurred within thirty years. From the late sixteenth century to the mid-eighteenth century, the quantity of slaves shipped across the Atlantic grew at an average rate of 2 percent per year. Driving this growing demand was the sugar plantation system, as Brazil came to be joined by Barbados, Jamaica, Martinique, and other colonies. By 1650 the New World had displaced the Middle East as the dominant destination of African slaves. During the final years of price stability in the seventeenth century, African suppliers developed efficient methods for delivering more slaves with no increase in cost. But, by the opening of the eighteenth century, the limits on the ability of Africans to provide cheap slaves had been reached, and prices rose dramatically. The cost of obtaining slaves rose as prospective captives learned to defend themselves better and as middlemen and toll collectors interposed themselves into the process of delivery. For these reasons as well as actual population decline, slaves became scarce relative to the level of demand. The price increases in this period led to the establishment of something resembling a world market for slave labor, in which New World demand and prices for slaves were so high that both slave prices and the quantity of slaves moved were affected not only along the western coast but in many regions of the African continent as well.

Two African regions bore the brunt of the expansion in exports at the turn of the eighteenth century: the Bight of Benin and the Gold Coast. Both of these regions experienced numerous wars among small states near the coast, from which captives were sold to the Europeans. For the Gold Coast, it meant the eclipse of gold as the main regional export for a time; for the Bight of Benin it brought entry into large-scale Atlantic trade. In both cases, the volume of slave exports rose within three decades to a level that reduced the region's population, after which slave exports declined slowly. Similar patterns of export increase to the limits of population tolerance, with a subsequent slow decline in exports, can be traced for other regions at other times. For Upper Guinea, the most substantial export of slaves occurred between 1600 and 1630. For the Senegambia, after a spurt of exports in the sixteenth century, exports rose again to a peak in the late seventeenth century. For the Bight of Biafra, slave exports shot up from the 1740s to the 1760s and remained at a high level through the 1820s. The Loango coast experienced a sharp increase in export volume in the years from 1720 to 1740 and another increase to a still higher volume from 1780 to 1800. Angola also experienced two great spurts in exports: one in the mid-seventeenth century, after which slave exports declined, and one during the 1720s to 1740s, after which exports remained at a high level into the nineteenth century.

Each of these sudden regional expansions in the slave trade caused—and reflected—changes in the methods and the morality of obtaining slaves. War, judicial procedures, and kidnapping were the main processes by which slaves were obtained—war predominated in most of West Africa, kidnapping predominated in the Bight of Biafra, and judicial procedures played a leading role in Central Africa. For the Gold Coast, Ray Kea has documented changes in the technology and social organization of war that preceded the expansion of slave exports there. As war was transformed from the combat of elites, with minimal and defensive war aims, to combat based on musketry, on the *levée en masse*, and on objectives of territorial conquest, a seemingly endless stream of conflicts and captives was unleashed. A similar transformation accompanied the rise of slave exports from the Bight of Benin.

Were the wars provoked by the desire to sell slaves, or were the captives simply a by-product of wars fought for other reasons? Observers of the slave trade have debated the question inconclusively ever since the Atlantic trade began. Philip Curtin posed this choice with an eye to sustaining the vision of emergent Africa: he contrasted a political model and an economic model for enslavement in the Senegambia and concluded that the evidence best supported the political model. E. Phillip LeVeen offered the economist's response. The decision to export slaves captured according to the political model depended on the level of prices, and thus slave exporting, as opposed to capturing, fits the economic model. The test of the issue is the responsiveness of slave export quantities to price changes. Even for small and well-defined areas, the elasticity of slave supply fluctuated sharply with passage of time. Much of the apparent disorder, however, can be resolved by distinguishing periods when the system of supply was stable and positive price-responsiveness was clear (1730 to 1800 in the Bight of Benin) from periods when the ability of merchants to supply slaves was either improving sharply (1740 to 1780 in the Bight of Biafra) or declining (1690 to 1730 in the Bight of Benin). These three examples can be set within the vision of Afrique engagée. In the Bight of Benin in the eighteenth century, domestic and external forces were locked in an equilibrium of sorts; in the Bight of Biafra in the mid-eighteenth century, domestic conditions changed more rapidly than can be explained by the influence of external forces alone; and in the Bight of Benin from the late seventeenth through the early eighteenth century external influences were the main source of African sociodemographic change.

As the demand for slaves continued to grow, opportunities for restrictive and monopolistic practices arose. Richard Nelson Bean, who has collected the best data on prices, joined with Robert Paul Thomas to argue that the Atlantic slave market was competitive and did not allow for monopoly profits, since European shippers could escape price gouging in one African port by going to another. The contrary position is based on the argument that, since European shippers required a speedy turn-around and good relations with their African suppliers, they were tied to a single port. Even without monopoly profits, however, some African slave exporters may have collected high rates of profit through economic rent—that is, those merchants who were able to obtain slaves at unusually low cost still sold them at the prevailing market price. The African revenues from slave exports, which rose along with prices at the turn of the eighteenth century, were almost all turned into expenditures on imported goods: the value and volume of these imports thus increased dramatically at the same time that export prices rose.

The sudden increases in mercantile profit and in the volume of imported goods simultaneously began to restrict African population size. The technique of using New World inventories of slaves to project the ethnic origins of slave exports has established that, for the Bight of Benin, slaves came almost entirely from the Aja-speaking peoples in and around the kingdom of Danhomè, near the coast. The full demographic drain on the Bight of Benin was concentrated on this group, which experienced a loss estimated at over 3 percent of the population each year for over forty consecutive years. This loss was sufficient to reduce the Aja population substantially over the course of a century, both in absolute terms and in relation to the surrounding ethnic groups, notably the Yoruba. . . .

The coastal exports of young adult slaves, twice as many men as women, tended to transform the structure of the population and the organization of society. A surplus of women developed, so that polygyny was reinforced, and work done by women in some places replaced that done by men. African traditions of family structure and division of labor, no matter how deeply instilled, could not but bend before these demographic pressures. The tradition of female agricultural labor in the matrilineal belt of Zaire and Angola may have been strengthened as an accommodation to the shortage of men for production. Similarly, although the institution of polygyny preceded the slave trade, its extent was reinforced by the surplus of women. In addition, a surplus of women meant that men did not need to wait until their late twenties and thirties to marry their first and second wives. Indeed, the fear of enslavement may have encouraged men to marry at a young age. . . .

The demand for slaves affected African polities by causing them not only to participate in slave exports but also to attempt to end it. The kingdom of Benin successfully withdrew from supplying slaves early in the sixteenth century. The Oyo Empire, though by reputation long tied to the slave trade, probably contributed only minimally to the export of slaves from Africa until late in the eighteenth century. And Boubacar Barry has interpreted the political events of the late seventeenth century in the Waalo kingdom of Senegal as an abortive attempt to withdraw from the slave trade. It is for the kingdom of Danhomè that the issue of attempted withdrawal from the slave trade has caused the most controversy. There is a certain plausibility to the notion that, in an area that was ravaged by trade in slaves and that experienced depopulation along with internecine wars, one state should attempt to conquer the whole region to end such conflicts and prevent social collapse. The question remains whether King Agaja's wars of the 1770s were an attempt to do so. But Danhomè's invasion and subjugation by the distant yet powerful Oyo made any such expanded Aja state impossible, and from 1730 to 1830 Danhomè faced a ring of weakened but by no means vanquished enemies; the internecine wars provided the New World with an inordinately large proportion of its slave laborers.

The case of Asante, to the west, represents a slightly different resolution of the same problem. Asante rose in the late seventeenth century to challenge Denkyira, the Gold Coast's dominant power, and eventually succeeded in incorporating virtually all the Twi-speaking peoples. As a result, the export of the people of Asante declined after about 1730, and the large number of slaves exported from the Gold Coast in succeeding years came increasingly from the interior Voltaic peoples. In Oyo, only with the constitutional crisis and a series of factional disputes that began in the 1770s did that kingdom's export slave trade become significant, and the magnitude of slave exports grew with the decay of the state. Thus, although the slave trade certainly affected politics, the nature of the trade's impact varied sharply from polity to polity; sometimes, as in the case of Oyo, politics influenced the trade in slaves more than the trade influenced internal affairs.

The aggregate demographic impact of the slave trade on Africa reached a peak in the late eighteenth century, when slave exports averaged some one hundred thousand per year, and this high level of export continued into the early nineteenth century. During this period, the foci of enslavement tended to move from west to east and from coast to interior. For this period, then, it is most appropriate to assert that slave exports diminished the African population.

One method of assessing the population drain on individual ethnic groups entails, as mentioned above, making a New World inventory of slaves' ethnic origins. A second approach focuses on whole regions, assessing the ability of regional populations to reproduce themselves in the face of the population drain resulting from slave exports. Roger Anstey, David Northrup, and, most effectively, John Thornton have used this procedure to good effect. Thornton's results indicate a decline in the population of the whole Congo-Angola region during the eighteenth century, and his analysis further suggests that, during the height of the export trade, most of the regions of the West African coast could have withstood the pressure from the trade in slaves only with difficulty. A third approach, continental in scope, has been adopted by Joseph Inikori. His method focuses not so much on the actual reduction in population as on the difference between the actual population of Africa and the counterfactual population that might have existed in the absence of slave exports.

Yet another approach involves the estimation of the impact of the slave trade through computer simulation. In this case, a model African population is postulated, divided into raiding and raided groups, and assigned a series of demographic and slave-trade rates: fertility, mortality, age-sex composition of the captured population, division of the captives between domestic and exported slaves, and so forth. Preliminary projections of the model's results suggest that the slave trade caused losses that, if not devastating to the continent, were certainly severe. For the western coast, a region with an estimated population of twenty-five million in 1700, some six million slaves left in the course of the eighteenth century. The total number enslaved is projected at some twelve million, with four million retained in domestic slavery and over two million lost to death in the course of enslavement. Under these conditions, the African population in 1800 was substantially less than it would have been in the absence of the trade in slaves. For the northern savanna and Horn, whose exports rarely exceeded twenty thousand per year, losses in slave exports were felt more acutely than the numbers alone suggest, because of the predominance of women exported. As a result, the northern savanna and the Horn were probably unable to experience any increase in population during the seventeenth and eighteenth centuries.

The demographic drain of the slave trade interacted with Africa's periodic droughts and famines. As the experience of the nineteenth century suggests, the incidence of drought and famine served at once to increase and to decrease slave exports. The onset of bad times caused the destitute to sell themselves or their children into slavery; but the decline in population resulting from famine tended to reduce the number of slaves. Stephen Baier and Paul E. Lovejoy have documented the great drought of the northern savanna in the mid-eighteenth century, which caused hardship, migration, and economic decline. Climatic recovery in the following decades led to economic growth, which was reflected both in the increase in slave exports and in the rise of the Sokoto Caliphate. Jill Dias and Joseph C. Miller have documented a cycle of drought, famine, and epidemic in Angola that severely limited population growth. These Malthusian checks on population provide the primary evidence for revising downward Inikori's estimates of the counterfactual African population: Africa's population would surely have been substantially greater without the slave trade, but to know how much so requires a better knowledge of the effects of famine and disease than we now have. Miller may, however, have gone too far in arguing that the limits imposed by disease and drought were so great that these factors, rather than the slave trade, provided the fundamental limits on Angola's population.

The selective export of women from the coastal regions had its greatest impact in the late eighteenth century. The results of the simulation model suggests [sic] that, while the sex ratio among those populations that lost slaves remained roughly equal, the proportion of adult women to men rose substantially for the western coast as a whole: the estimated ratio of adult women to men rose to roughly six to five among the raiding populations. But in those areas with the heaviest participation in slave exporting, the disparity in the sex ratio became greater. John Thornton's analysis of the Portuguese censuses for Angola indicates that the ratio of adult women to men was as much as two to one. On the one hand, this sex ratio shows how African societies could attempt to cope with an enormous drain on the population with losing their ability to reproduce; the people of Angola virtually became a livestock herd to be harvested. On the other, one woman was exported for every two to three men, and the loss of the women's reproductive potential made it all the more difficult for the population to maintain itself. The bulk of the agricultural labor fell on the women who remained in Angola, and the incidence of polygyny remained high. . . .

By the mid-nineteenth century, a dramatic reversal in the character of the Atlantic slave trade had taken place. Most New World areas had dropped out of the slave trade, and slave imports were illegal in the remaining areas of demand—Cuba and Brazil. As a result, although the prices of slaves in the New World rose because of the scarcity of new imports, the export demand for slaves at any given price on the African coast had fallen significantly, and the price of slaves in Africa fell almost as significantly. The relatively scarce price data available for the early nineteenth century are somewhat contradictory, so the precise timing of the price decline remains to be confirmed. But it is clear that, sometime between 1780 and 1850, the price of slaves on the African coast fell, in real terms, by one-half. The mechanisms of slave supply remained in place, however, so that a glut on the slave market became evident. This nineteenth-century glut brought a pervasive change in the character of African slavery: as slaves, particularly male slaves, came within the purchasing power of African buyers, the scope of African slavery expanded greatly in the mid-nineteenth century, although the total number of people captured may not have changed greatly.

As more women remained in Africa, the number of births dramatically increased; and, as more men stayed, the previous drain of the adult male population ended, although the process of enslavement for the African market still implied a significant mortality. These changes resulted in rapid population growth. In addition, the large number of cheap male slaves now made the situation on the coast much more like that in the savanna, where male slaves were used for agricultural labor. Thus the coastal areas now developed slave plantations that produced for palace populations, for the African market, and for export. The mid-nineteenth-century growth in the export of palm oil, coffee, and peanuts thus reflected not only the rise in European demand for these products but also a significant decline in the cost of production because of the fall in slave prices. . . .

Ethnographers of the early twentieth century, writing in the last days of [African] slavery, described the institution as relatively benign, emphasizing the legal and societal protections available to slaves as well as their potential for upward mobility. These reports—written after slave raiding and the trade in slaves had ceased and after slaveholders had lost the support of the state—stand in sharp contrast to the travelers' reports of the late nineteenth century, which tell of brutal raids, immense loss of life, and massive exploitation of slaves by masters. Each of these views of African slavery was appropriate to the precise time at which it was written. Both views, but particularly the former, have in turn been taken by subsequent scholars as appropriate characterizations of African slavery across the centuries.

The vision of emergent Africa, based on the assumed existence of continuous pressures for change within African societies, tends to suggest that both of these static views of servile institutions were invalid, without posing an alternative. The vision of Afrique engagée, by explicitly reintroducing external forces of causation into a framework that assumes an African dynamism not only confirms that suggestion but indicates the nature and timing of some important African social changes. In so doing, this historiographical approach must admit to a range in the type of interactions. In some cases, domestic forces dominated the interactions; the expansion and transformation of polygyny under the influence of the slave trade, for example, took place in the context of a previous African attachment to multiple marriage. In other cases, external forces dominated the interaction; both depopulation and the impact of imported goods, for instance, represent the domination of outside influences. And the precise combination of domestic and external forces provided the key impetus to certain changes, notably in the rise of Asante and Danhomè, the collapse of Kongo, and the mutual reinforcement of the slave trade, famine, and epidemic.

The return on this increased complexity in analytical framework is a clearer time-perspective on African society: African slavery, along with a range of associated institutions, underwent successive transformations in the seventeenth, eighteenth, and nineteenth centuries under the impact of changing economic, demographic, and political conditions. Suzanne Miers and Igor Kopytoff, in an essay that sits firmly within the emergent Africa tradition of analysis, have gone so far as to criticize the use of the term "slavery" in Africa on the grounds that it implies a greater uniformity in African institutions of servitude than is warranted. Their emphasis on the specificity, in sociological cross-section, of African systems of slavery is valid in principle if somewhat exaggerated in practice. To their sociological specificity must be added, however, the specificity of African societies in historical time-perspective, as they changed through the action of the diverse creative powers within them and the varying external pressures upon them. In the era of the slave trade, the external influences were so powerful as to set in motion comparable trends in social change in many parts of the African continent two centuries before the colonial conquest did in a vastly different fashion.

John Thornton

Africa's Effects on the Slave Trade

The most recent excerpt (this volume's second from John Thornton's book) accepts that Africa suffered serious demographic damage from the slave trade, but Thornton is less willing than Manning to blame external factors for Africa's social ills and is quite unwilling to accept Rodney's underdevelopment thesis. Instead, Thornton argues that Africans participated in the slave trade willingly, with full understanding, and from a position of strength. He suggests that in many places a preexisting trade in slaves was simply diverted into the Atlantic.

The success of Africans in resisting the early European attempts at raiding their coasts meant that the interactions that would follow would be largely peaceful and commercial—for it would not be until 1579 that a major war would develop, in Angola, and even there it rapidly became an indecisive standstill. There would be no dramatic European conquests in Africa, and even the slaves who would flood the South Atlantic and sustain colonization in America would be purchased more often than captured. This state of affairs was already being put in place by [the Portuguese] expeditions in 1456–62 and would characterize relations between Europeans and Africans for centuries to come.

African naval victories might not necessarily guarantee that the commerce that grew up in place of raiding was truly under African control or necessarily served their interests (or the interests of the wealthy

John Thornton, "Africa's Effects on the Slave Trade" from *Africa and Africans in the Making of the Atlantic World, 1400–1800,* 1992, 1998, pp. 43–45, 53, 66–69, 72–75, 94–97. Reprinted by permission of Cambridge University Press.

and powerful in African society). Indeed, many scholars in recent years have most often seen the commerce of Atlantic Africa with Europeans as destructive and unequal, with Europeans reaping most of the long-range profits and Africans unable to benefit or being forced, through commercial weakness, into accepting trade that ultimately placed Africa in its current situation of dependency and underdevelopment.

Perhaps the most influential scholar to advocate such a position was Walter Rodney, whose work on Africa's Atlantic trade concluded that the commerce with Europe was a first, decisive step in the under-development of Africa. As Rodney saw it, this was because Africa was at a lower level of economic development than Europe and was thus forced into a sort of "colonial" trade in which Africans gave up raw materials and human resources (in the form of slaves) in exchange for manufactured goods—a form of dependency that certainly character-izes modern African trade. . . .

An examination of African economic development by 1500 and the exact nature of the Atlantic trade, however, does not support this pessimistic position. Africans played a more active role in developing the commerce, and they did so on their own initiative. On the one hand, the Atlantic trade was not nearly as critical to the African economy as these scholars believed, and on the other hand, African manufacturing was more than capable of handling competition from preindustrial Europe.

In order to understand the role of the African economy in the Atlantic trade we need to examine two related issues, both of which are raised in the works of scholars who see Africans as junior and dependent trading partners. First is the assumption of African backwardness in manufacturing, based largely on the analogy with Africa's present lack of manufacturing capacity and its impact on modern African econo-mies. Second is the assumption of commercial domination, in which Europeans somehow were able to control the market for African goods, either through monopoly or through commercial manipulation of some other sort. . . .

Europe exported a wide range of goods to Africa before 1650, of which we can recognize several categories. First and surely foremost in terms of volume was cloth—a whole world of textiles of dozens of types by the seventeenth century. Then there were metal goods, principally iron and copper, in raw (iron bars and copper manillas) and worked form (knives, swords, copper basins and bowls, etc.). Next there was currency, consisting of tons of cowry shells. This trade was especially important in Benin and the Slave Coast though shells were also imported into central Africa. Finally there is what we might describe as nonutilitarian items, such as jewelry (beads for the most part), mechanical toys and curiosities, and alcoholic beverages.

What is significant about all of these items is that none were "essential commodities." Africa had well-developed industries producing every single item on the list, and although not all of them were produced in every district, a substantial number of these items were imported into regions where there was clearly no pressing need, in a strictly functional sense, to import them.

It was, in short, not to meet African needs that the trade developed or even to make up for shortfalls in production or failures in quality of the African manufactures. Rather, Africa's trade with Europe was largely moved by prestige, fancy, changing taste, and a desire for variety—and such whimsical motivations were backed up by a relatively well developed productive economy and substantial purchasing power. The Atlantic trade of Africa was not simply motivated by the filling of basic needs, and the propensity to import on the part of Africans was not simply a measure of their need or inefficiency, but instead, it was a measure of the extent of their domestic market. . . .

In the end, then, the European trade with Africa can scarcely be seen as disruptive in itself, for it did not oust any line of African production, nor did it thwart development by providing items through trade that might have otherwise been manufactured in Africa, even if one differentiates, say, high-quality cloth from low or high-grade steel from low. There was no reason, therefore, that Africans should have wanted to stop the trade, or that their desire to continue it was based on necessity. . . .

It is fairly clear . . . that European merchants, whether acting under the direction of states or companies, were unable to monopolize the trade of Africa. It is just as clear that African states, although attempting the same sort of thing, were ultimately no more successful. No African state ever really dominated the trade of any part of the African coast. African sovereignty was just as fragmented as the theoretical sovereignty that Europeans tried to maintain over the trade.

However, the African states did help to balance whatever economies of scale individual European merchants or companies may have had. Thus, it might be argued that a well-capitalized European merchant could have taken economic advantage, at least in the short run, of intense competition between hundreds of African traders. The African states' role in commerce limited this effect, however, thus offsetting whatever advantages a shipper's scale of operations might have afforded.

State requirements put a great number of legal and technical obstacles between European merchants and African buyers, as well as making the state itself a regular participant in the trade. A Dutch commercial guide of about 1655, for example, records the gifts and taxes that had to be paid in a variety of countries along the "Slave Coast" area from the Volta to Cameroon. Those at Allada were perhaps the most complicated, although perhaps only because the writer of the guide (apparently resident in São Tomé) understood them best. There, the prospective buyer of slaves and cloth from Allada had to present a complex series of presents to dancers, food sellers, linguists, brokers, Allada nobles, and the king himself, both upon arrival and upon departure. That such a system was not unique to Allada is clearly shown in the variety of customs the guide describes at Benin, Calabar, the Niger delta, and the Gabon region. . . .

These negotiations, which were often time-consuming and which many Europeans visitors thought to complain of, were essentially a manifestation of the insistence on the part of authorities in African states that they benefit first and certainly from trade. They were often willing to provide return gifts, sometimes of substantial value, after customs were paid . . . as a way of making a special connection between themselves and the European with whom they were trading. But typically their desire was to ensure that they received first choice of the best goods and the best price, which perhaps constituted a second tax that went along with the gifts that made up the customs charges. . . .

But after African rulers had insisted on involving their sovereign rights to control trade or guarantee their profits, they were usually content to allow trade to take place freely once they had received their share. But very often even this trade was far from being the commercial free-for-all of a real market. This was because although African states allowed private trade, they played a major role in determining which Africans would be able to trade. The African bourgeoisie, like their counterparts in Europe, thrived largely because the state supported their position, and in many ways they used this patronage to their advantage. . . .

If Africans were experienced traders and were not somehow dominated by European merchants due to European market control or some superiority in manufacturing or trading techniques, then we can say confidently that Africa's commercial relationship with Europe was not unlike international trade anywhere in the world of the period. But historians have balked at this conclusion because they believe that the slave trade, which was an important branch of Afro-European commerce from the beginning, should not be viewed as a simple commodity exchange. After all, slaves are also a source of labor, and at least to some extent, their removal from Africa represented a major loss to Africa. The sale of slaves must therefore have been harmful to Africa, and African decisions to sell must have been forced or involuntary for one or more reasons.

The idea of the slave trade as a harmful commerce is especially supported by the work of historical demographers. Most who have studied the question of the demographic consequences of the trade have reached broad agreement that the trade was demographically damaging from a fairly early period, especially when examined from a local or regional (as opposed to a continental) perspective. In addition to the net demographic drain, which began early in some areas (like Angola), the loss of adult males had potentially damaging impacts on sex ratios, dependency rates, and perhaps the sexual division of labor.

In addition to these demographic effects, historians interested in social and political history have followed Walter Rodney in arguing that the slave trade caused social disruption (such as increasing warfare and related military damage), adversely altered judicial systems, or increased inequality. Moreover, Rodney argued that the slave trade increased the numbers of slaves being held in Africa and intensified their exploitation, a position that Paul Lovejoy, its most recent advocate, calls the "transformation thesis." Because of this perception of a widespread negative impact, many scholars have argued that the slave trade, if not other forms of commerce, must have been forced on unwilling African participants, perhaps through the type of commercial inequities that we have already discussed or perhaps through some sort of military pressure. . . .

When Rodney presented his conclusions on the negative impact and hence special status of the slave trade as a branch of trade, it was quickly contested by J. D. Fage, and more recently, the transformation thesis has been attacked by David Eltis. As these scholars see it, slavery was widespread and indigenous in African society, as was, naturally enough, a commerce in slaves. Europeans simply tapped this existing market, and Africans responded to the increased demand over the centuries by providing more slaves. The demographic impact, although important, was local and difficult to disentangle from losses due to internal wars and slave trading on the domestic African market. In any case, the decision makers who allowed the trade to continue, whether merchants or political leaders, did not personally suffer the larger-scale losses and were able to maintain their operations. Consequently, one need not accept that they were forced into participation against their will or made decisions irrationally.

The evidence for the period before 1680 generally supports this second position. Slavery was widespread in Africa, and its growth and development were largely independent of the Atlantic trade, except that insofar as the Atlantic commerce stimulated internal commerce and development it also led to more widespread holding of slaves. The Atlantic slave trade was the outgrowth of this internal slavery. Its demographic impact, however, even in the early stages was significant, but the people adversely affected by this impact were not the ones making the decisions about participation. . . .

Thus, . . . the slave trade (and the Atlantic trade in general) should not be seen as an "impact" brought in from outside and functioning as some sort of autonomous factor in African history. Instead, it grew out of and was rationalized by the African societies who participated in it and had complete control over it until the slaves were loaded onto European ships for transfer to Atlantic societies.

The reason that slavery was widespread in Africa was not, as some have asserted, because Africa was an economically underdeveloped region in which forced labor had not yet been replaced by free labor. Instead, slavery was rooted in deep-seated legal and institutional structures of African societies, and it functioned quite differently from the way it functioned in European societies. . . .

Thus slaves could be found in all parts of Atlantic Africa, performing all sorts of duties. When Europeans came to Africa and offered to buy slaves, it is hardly surprising that they were almost immediately accepted. Not only were slaves found widely in Africa, but the area had a well-developed slave trade, as evidenced by the numbers of slaves in private hands. Anyone who had the wherewithal could obtain slaves from the domestic market, though sometimes it required royal or state permission, as in the Gold Coast. Europeans could tap this market just as any African could.

Moreover, the most likely owners of slaves—wealthy merchants and state officials or rulers—were exactly the people with whom European traders came into contact. Because merchants selling gold, ivory products, mats, copper bracelets, pepper, or any other trade commodity in Africa would also be interested in the buying and selling of slaves, European merchants could readily find sources. This was not so much because Africans were inveterate slave dealers, as it was because the legal basis for wealth in Africa lay in the idea of transferring ownership of people. This legal structure made slavery and slave marketing widespread and created secondary legal mechanisms for securing and regulating the sale of slaves, which Europeans could use as well as Africans.

The significance of African slavery in the development of the slave trade can be clearly seen in the remarkable speed with which the continent began exporting slaves. As soon as the Portuguese had reached the Senegal region and abandoned their early strategy of raiding for commerce, 700–1,000 slaves were exported per year, . . . reaching as many as 1,200–2,500 slaves per year by the end of the century. . . . The reason that such dramatic numbers were reached immediately may indicate nothing more . . . than that a preexisting engagement with foreign markets was transferred to Atlantic ones. Most of the early European slave trading with West Africa, even that with such relatively remote regions as Benin and the Niger delta, known in the sixteenth century as the "River of Slaves," was simply an internal trade diverted to the Atlantic. . . .

That existing internal use and commerce in slaves lay behind the export trade is even more strongly suggested by the trade of central Africa. Unlike the West African trade, which drew on an ancient slave trade with North Africa and might thus have already been affected by external contacts, the central African region had no such external links. Nevertheless, the king of Portugal regarded Kongo as sufficiently important a potential exporter of slaves that he granted settlers in São Tomé privileges to engage in the slave trade in 1493, just a few years after the development of official trade there. . . . Unfortunately we possess no early statistics for the volume of this trade, but . . . around 1507, in addition to some 2,000 slaves working on sugar plantations, the island held 5,000–6,000 slaves awaiting reexport. Presumably these slaves were recent imports who had probably arrived within the last year, and certainly half, but probably the majority, originated in central Africa. . . .

Slaves from central Africa were so numerous that they soon exceeded the capacity of São Tomé and the Mina trade to absorb them, and so they began the long journey to European markets. . . . Thus, at some point, probably within twenty years of first contact, central Africa was able to supply exports of slaves equal to the entire exports of West Africa. Clearly this sort of volume could not simply have been the occasional export of odd misfits. Nor have we any reason to believe that the Portuguese were able to either acquire the slaves themselves (except as clients of the Kongo kings) or force the Kongo to obtain the export slaves against their will. Instead, the growth of Kongo's trade had to draw on a well-developed system of slavery, slave marketing, and slave delivery that preexisted any European contact.

We must therefore conclude that the Atlantic slave trade and African participation in it had solid origins in African societies and legal systems. The institution of slavery was widespread in Africa and accepted in all the exporting regions, and the capture, purchase, transport, and sale of slaves was a regular feature of African society. This preexisting social arrangement was thus as much responsible as any external force for the development of the Atlantic slave trade.

Map 2. The Americas in the Era of the Slave Trade (showing places mentioned in the text).

PART

V Effects in the Americas and Europe

VARIETY OF OPINION

In at least two important areas of New World slavery, South Carolina and the eastern Amazon in Brazil, planters adopted African expertise in rice farming.

JUDITH A. CARNEY

. . . in the case of the peoples from the rice-growing areas of Africa taken to the early [Carolina] lowcountry and Amazonia, the numbers are so small . . . that the continued acceptance of the "black rice" argument is problematic.

DAVID ELTIS, PHILIP MORGAN, DAVID RICHARDSON

The triangular trade made an enormous contribution to Britain's industrial development. . . . But this industrial development . . . later outgrew mercantilism and destroyed it.

ERIC WILLIAMS

119

> . . . an ideology of free labor that would be understood in conflicting
> ways by workers and employers [in Britain] nevertheless . . . unite[d]
> them in condemning chattel slavery in distant colonies.
>
> DAVID BRION DAVIS

Judith A. Carney

The African Roots of American Rice

Many recent studies have emphasized the impact that millions of Africans
had in the Americas. In this selection from her book, *Black Rice*, UCLA
geographer Judith Carney argues that people from rice-growing areas of
Africa have not been given proper credit for their roles in the development
of rice cultivation in the Americas.

. . . Of the more than twenty species of the rice genus *Oryza*, only two
were domesticated, *glaberrima* and *sativa*. Most likely both types were
introduced to the New World in the century following the voyages of
Columbus. The conventional interpretation of rice history in the Americas assigns Europeans the role of ingeniously adapting a crop of Asian
origin to New World conditions. This perspective, however, ignores the
role of Africans in establishing a preferred food staple under slavery.
The development of rice culture marked not simply the movement of
a crop across the Atlantic but also the transfer of an entire cultural system, from production to consumption.

Drawing upon diverse historical and botanical materials, I argue for
the primacy of African rice and skills in the crop's development in the
Americas. My focus is on treating the transfer of rice as the diffusion of an

indigenous knowledge system. The method involves a close inspection of the agricultural strategy of rice growing and its techniques—an agrarian genealogy—and their evolution over time. A knowledge system long practiced in West Africa was brought with slaves across the Atlantic. This book draws attention to how its diffusion has been misunderstood and misinterpreted in ways that diminished the significance of the African origins of the crop and of the people who grew the rice, processed the grain, and prepared the food. Recovery of this African knowledge system promotes our understanding of rice history in the Atlantic basin and the African contribution to the Americas. An agrarian genealogy of rice demands an intellectual journey through the Atlantic basin that reverses the direction of slaves across the Middle Passage.

The past several decades have witnessed an increasing willingness by scholars to concede that Africans may have played a significant role in shaping the cultures of the Americas since 1500. Among the longstanding themes in African-American history is the debate over cultural survival and acculturation. This dates to the early twentieth century, when anthropologist Melville Herskovits first tried to show that to believe that the African and the African-American had no past was to perpetuate a pernicious myth. In his 1941 book, *The Myth of the Negro Past*, Herskovits challenged the notion of sociologist E. Franklin Frazier and his students that slavery had stripped its victims of their African heritage. Over the next decades Herskovits and his followers identified various cultural retentions they viewed as African, particularly in relation to religion, language, and the arts. Much of this research, however, drew criticism for treating Africa as a single cultural area, a concept of culture very much in fashion at that time, but inaccurate in portraying the diversity and complexity of cultures found in just West Africa alone. The search for vestiges of an African culture in the United States consequently proved so generalized that it provided little understanding of the distinctive black cultures that formed in the Americas. Nonetheless, Herskovits's field research in West Africa, the Caribbean, and Suriname made him the first scholar to examine populations of African descent from a perspective focused on the Atlantic basin.

Rejecting the value of identifying African traits for explaining the distinctive black cultures of the Americas, anthropologists Sidney Mintz and Richard Price emphasized instead the process of cultural change. In *The Birth of African-American Culture: An Anthropological Perspective* (1976) they argued that cultural fragmentation and the formation of plantation societies of slaves from disparate ethnic origins resulted in syncretic cultures. Slaves survived the brutal and dehumanizing experience of bondage by developing hybrid cultures. Enslavement thus forced them to create their own culture within a setting where plantation owners exercised an absolute monopoly of power. The social experience of being African and a slave, Mintz and Price argued, proved far more significant in structuring the black cultures of the Americas than any traits or retentions associated with specific African ethnic groups. The emphasis of Mintz and Price on the syncretic cultures slaves shaped from their African origins profoundly influenced studies of black cultures throughout the African diaspora.

Until the 1970s interest in the role that Africa, and West Africa in particular, may have played in the shaping of certain aspects of society and culture in the Americas remained largely a concern of anthropologists. This changed profoundly in 1974 when historian Peter Wood published *Black Majority*. In a radical departure from previous studies of the coastal South Carolina plantation economy, Wood moved blacks from the background to the center of the analysis by showing the context in which slaves of different ethnic groups forged a new way of life around the cultivation of rice. He argued that the emergence of rice as the chief plantation crop owed a great deal to the fact that many West Africans, unlike the European colonists, grew rice before crossing the Middle Passage of slavery. Wood's brilliant insight was to emphasize the skills that Africans brought to the Carolina frontier through a critical reading of early accounts of rice cultivation, written by slave owners, that attributed such knowledge to European ingenuity. His work shifted the research emphasis from cultural *change* to cultural *exchange* while challenging the long-held notion that slaves contributed only unskilled labor to the plantation economies of the Americas.

Historian Daniel C. Littlefield's book, *Rice and Slaves*, published in 1981, added several innovative directions to Wood's research. In the spirit of Herskovits, Littlefield placed his analysis of Carolina rice origins within the context of the Atlantic basin, identifying the area of West Africa where rice was planted and thus the geographic origin of ethnic groups familiar with its cultivation during the Atlantic slave trade. He documented the preference among rice planters for slaves from specific ethnic groups, thereby revealing their awareness of those skilled in rice cultivation. Drawing upon evidence from shipping accounts and newspaper ads for runaways, Littlefield contended that planters were aware of ethnic differences among Africans. Documentation shows that plantation owners, even if not always able to obtain Africans skilled in rice growing, sought to use this knowledge of rice cultivation for their own purposes.

The emphasis of Wood and Littlefield on the diffusion of skills from West Africa to South Carolina in rice cultivation explored new terrain. Instead of examining the impact of one culture upon another, they emphasized how Africans from diverse ethnicities, thrown together in slavery, created a new way of life in coastal Carolina, where a crop known only to some of them became the plantation staple. The association of agricultural skills with certain African ethnicities within a specific geographic region opened up provocative questions concerning the black Atlantic and called for a research perspective emphasizing not only culture but also culture in relationship to technology and the environment.

A perspective on culture and environment in Atlantic history was already being developed by historian Alfred W. Crosby in his book *The Columbian Exchange*, published in 1972, as well as in other volumes that appeared over the following decade. Emphasis on the cultural and biological exchanges that radically transformed New and Old World ecosystems in the aftermath of the voyages of Columbus served as Crosby's point of departure. His work chronicled the transatlantic exchange of peoples, plants, animals, and germs, drawing particular attention to the impact of seeds of New World origin on the Old World, and the role of Europeans in their global diffusion. Crosby's original notion of this "Columbian Exchange" has become central to our understanding of the transoceanic plant exchanges that accompanied European voyages across the globe. An enduring legacy of his research was to place culture and environment in a new relationship through the dramatic transformations that occurred in Atlantic world ecosystems.

The exchange of plants of African origin and the plausible role of slaves in their adaptation to New World environments, however, has only recently begun to receive consideration among researchers. Much of this neglect has derived from the racial and gender biases of so much inherited scholarship, which cast Africa as a backwater of the global economic system, intrinsically devoid of civilization. As bondage placed males and females in the social category of slaves, scholarship dispossessed them of their preexisting ethnic and gendered forms of knowledge, robbing them of their real contributions to the Americas. African food systems, the foundation of civilization, were similarly ignored. The historical botany of West Africa's chief food staple, rice, for instance, was not widely known in the anglophone world until the 1970s. The question of whether slaves brought with them any inherited knowledge and skills from the African continent would await the research of Peter Wood and others.

Although the research of Wood and Littlefield has chipped away at the notion that slaves brought few skills across the Middle Passage, those contributions are still too frequently conceptualized as minor. Little ground in fact has given way over the issue that slaves may have transferred crucial technologies to the Americas, such as milling devices or systems of water control for irrigation. Consideration of this proposition strikes deep into the widely held belief in Western culture that attributes the political-economic hegemony of Europe and the United States to a preeminent mastery of technology, which in turn distinguishes Europe and its culture from all other societies. In this view the direction of technology and its advanced diffuses across geographic space to non-European peoples. . . .

This book draws attention to the knowledge system underlying the cultivation of rice in the Americas and West Africa. It investigates not only food and cultural identity but issues of indigenous knowledge and epistemology, human agency and social structure, seed transfers and the diffusion of cropping systems, agricultural innovation, and the power relations that shape agrarian practices. An examination of these issues in the context of rice history in the Americas demands rethinking the meaning of the Columbian Exchange to include not only the seeds that transferred throughout the Atlantic basin but the cropping systems as well. People and plants together migrated as a result of European global expansion. And among these were millions of Africans whose enslavement forced them to become involuntary migrants to the Americas. Rice figured crucially among the seeds that accompanied their migration, slaves planted the crop wherever social and environmental conditions seemed propitious. In adapting a favored dietary staple to local conditions, slaves drew upon a sophisticated knowledge system that informed cultivation and processing methods. Such practices in West Africa have long been ethnic and gendered. This indigenous African expertise mediated the diffusion of rice cultivation to the Americas and offered a means to negotiate the terms of labor in slavery. . . .

Considerations of prior knowledge and its geographical basis, unfortunately, and not yet a central concern for understanding the significance of the global plant dispersals of the Columbian Exchange. In fact, emphasis on seed transfers has inadvertently removed the knowledge systems developed by specific peoples from the agricultural history of areas revolutionized by the plants they domesticated. The emphasis on seeds over the cropping systems as they diffused throughout the Atlantic world consequently fails to reveal the ethnic and gendered dimensions of indigenous knowledge, which figure importantly in this account of the early history of rice cultivation in the Americas. In disregarding the techniques and processing methods that developed in specific geographical regions with plant domestication, agricultural history is reduced to the mere exchange of seeds by the group brokering their transfer, thereby privileging that group by attributing to it the ingenuity in "discovering" the principles of cultivation. In the case of rice, this position has resulted in a serious distortion that has obscured African technological contributions to rice culture in the Americas, especially where the crop was grown under submersion. Tracing the diffusion of agrarian practices, water control, winnowing, milling, and the cooking techniques associated with African rice cultivation across the Middle Passage to the Americas enables us to place ingenuity in its proper setting, that is, with the West African slaves already skilled in the crop's cultivation.

The establishment of rice cultivation characterized most regions settled by slaves or runaways in the Americas and attests to the crop's significance for cultural identity. In much of West Africa to this day, a meal is not considered complete unless served with rice. The cereal figures importantly in cultural traditions and ritual, and its pounding for consumption even marks the passage of time, as women's rhythmic striking of a pestle against a mortar full of rice grains heralds the beginning of a new day in countless villages of the region. But woven in complex ways with issues of identity is a deep understanding of how to grow rice in diverse habitats and to adapt the crop to challenging environmental circumstances. Rice is a knowledge system that represents ingenuity as well as enormous toil. In at least two important areas of New World slavery, South Carolina and the eastern Amazon in Brazil, planters adopted African expertise in rice farming to develop plantations based on the crop. In South Carolina where slaves' endeavors succeeded, knowledge of rice cultivation likely afforded them some leverage to negotiate the conditions of their labor. This book seeks to

move beyond the imagery of the black Uncle Ben promoting the converted rice sold in U.S. markets to place that rice and his ancestors in
their rightful historical context.

David Eltis, Philip Morgan, and David Richardson

Problems with the "Black Rice" Thesis

The thesis about "black rice" was roundly attacked by three distinguished
historians of the Atlantic: American historian Philip Morgan of Johns
Hopkins University and two major compilers of the monumental slave trade
database (Part 3), David Eltis and David Richardson. As the selection makes
clear, they do not seek to return to a tradition that exaggerated European
cultural contributions but insist that arguments about African contributions
must be consistent with the evidence and must employ sophisticated models of cultural migration.

Broadly speaking, two contrasting models dominate interpretations of
Atlantic history. One draws on Old World influences to explain the nature of societies and cultures in the Americas, while the other assigns
primacy to the New World environment. One stresses continuities, the
other change. The polar extremes are persistence and transience, inheritance and experience. An emphasis on inheritance prioritizes the
cultural baggage that migrants brought with them, whereas a focus on
experience highlights the physical and social environments, such as
climate, natural resources, and settlement processes, that they encountered. In modern parlance, one approach focuses on folkways, the other
on factor endowments. . . .

Atlantic history has matured to the point where it needs to break
out of the straitjacket imposed by the two models that have dominated

David Eltis, Philip Morgan, and David Richardson, "Agency and Diaspora in Atlantic
History," *American Historical Review* vol. 112, no. 5, December 2007, pp. 1329–33,
1353–58. Reprinted by permission of the authors and University of Chicago Press.

interpretations of the historiography of the Americas. There is no need either to choose between them or to pass judgment on their appropriateness. Rather than either Old World folkways or New World environments, we need to encompass both and become much more thoroughly Atlantic. Community and cultural formation in the early Americas was a product of many forces. Rather than frame the issues as solely one of transfers and conduits, we should also think of transformations and overlapping circuits. Rather than posit that slaves and planters always acted knowingly, we should entertain the possibility that they often responded to unseen market forces. Rather than assume that migrants remained conservatively attached to traditional ways, we might also view them as experimenters and improvisers. Once such a perspective is adopted, assigning agency becomes a complex and ambiguous task. But only then are we likely to generate an accurate and plausible picture of the foundation of Atlantic societies.

Since the 1970s, what can be termed the "black rice hypothesis" has emerged in ever stronger form in successive books by Peter H. Wood, Daniel C. Littlefield, and Judith A. Carney. The major export crop of eighteenth-century South Carolina and Georgia—rice—is now seen as predominantly a creation of Africans. This African contribution to New World agriculture is epitomized by the arresting title of Carney's book: *Black Rice*. A direct role for Africans in American history strikes a chord at a time when the national story is becoming less parochial and is increasingly being viewed in an Atlantic or global context. Furthermore, the emphasis on African agency resonates with histories from the bottom up and with subaltern studies in general. That South Carolina's rice industry was built not just on slave labor, but also on the slaves' agricultural and technological knowledge, is an exciting and appealing revelation. In a multicultural world, it is reassuring to realize that the black contribution to American life involved more than just backbreaking muscle power. The development of American rice culture, the claim goes, marked the transatlantic migration not only of an important crop but of an "entire cultural system." It was a major African accomplishment.

The basic argument rests on three core elements. First, rice culture was indigenous to Africa and was a practice of long standing. Well before the Europeans arrived, West Africans had developed complex systems of mangrove or tidal flood-plain, coastal estuarine, and upland rain-fed forms of rice cultivation. The area of greatest rice specialization centered on the Upper Guinea Coast, that part of the African littoral stretching for present-day Senegal to Liberia, but also reached into the interior, and by the seventeenth century may have extended coastwise to the western Gold Coast. Second, in contrast to the cultivation of most plantation crops in the Americas, notably sugar and tobacco, there was never a period when free—or at least non-slave—labor could be induced to produce rice for export. The workforce engaged in cultivating rice for export was always black, although elsewhere in the world, slave labor was not the norm. Moreover, among communities of Maroon or runaway slaves, rice seems to have often become the major staple and assumed special significance. Finally, putative parallels have emerged between rice cultivation in Africa and its counterparts in the Americas. From land preparation through sowing, weeding, irrigating, threshing, milling, winnowing, and cooking, African practices seemingly left a deep imprint on New World ways of growing and processing the crop.

South Carolina . . . was the primary, but not the only, rice producer in the Americas. By the late eighteenth century, northeastern Brazil . . . had become a significant center of slave-grown rice for export. There were, then, two key nodal points for commercial rice production in the eighteenth-century Americas, although one was much larger than the other. . . .

If the association of black labor and rice growing now seems widely accepted, the linkage between the rice-growing regions of Africa and those in the Americas is actually tenuous. Such a connection rests on some key claims, all related to flows of enslaved labor from parts of Africa to the Americas. First, and most obvious, Africans from rice-growing areas are said to have been either a significant minority or even a majority of those slaves arriving in New World regions that special-ized in rice. Planter preference is largely seen to have shaped slave ship-ments, at least to those areas that cultivated rice commercially. Second, African agricultural expertise was highly gendered. In some places, rice was solely a women's crop; in others—usually where more elaborate sys-tems arose for irrigating rice, requiring ditching and banking—a com-plex division of labor between men and women emerged; but in West Africa, women selected and sowed the seed and later processed and cooked the cereal. Given female expertise, it is claimed, slaves arrivals in South Carolina included a higher percentage of women than arriv-als in the Caribbean, where sugar was the predominant crop. Third, female slaves bound for American rice-growing areas allegedly com-manded higher prices than in other plantation economies. In South

Carolina, according to Carney, the labor of female slaves "was valued more on a par with that of male bondsmen than in the slave markets of the West Indies."

Such claims, if valid, would provide a prima facie case for the transfer of African rice-cultivating technologies to the Americas. But they have wider significance, too. With respect to gender, they represent an important caveat to the received wisdom that in the transatlantic traffic, male slaves typically outnumbered, and fetched higher prices than, females. As for commercial rice cultivation in the Americas, they seem to imply African acceptance of or even collaboration with—rather than resistance to—plantation development. At the very least, slaves are depicted as using their rice skills as a bargaining chip in active negotiation with masters. Suggestions, therefore, that rice cultivation in the Americas hinged upon the transfer of rice-growing skills and technologies through the slave trade from Africa challenge some of our most fundamental assumptions about African agency, the patterns and structures of transatlantic slavery, and working conditions on slave plantations. The degree of the African contribution to the development of American rice cultivation therefore merits close investigation.

There is no doubt that African slaves were the primary cultivators of rice and that some introduced Old World customs of sowing, threshing, and winnowing the crop into the New World. However, there is no compelling evidence that African slaves transferred whole agricultural systems to the New World; nor were they the primary players in creating and maintaining rice regimes in the Americas. Rather, a complex set of factors explains the operation of both the slave trade and the plantation system. Critical to the former were African supply conditions, Atlantic trade routes, and mercantile strategies, and to the latter, planter priorities, environmental conditions, and managerial initiatives. In neither case should the primary engine of development be reduced to planter preferences in the one and slave agency in the other.

A review of the African coastal provenance of slaves arriving in North America lends little support to the idea that rice planters sought slaves from the rice-growing regions of Africa. In the crucial formative period, prior to 1750, when the foundations of the lowcountry rice economy were laid and when slaves with rice-growing skills might have been expected to be in most demand, only about one-fifth of the region's Africans came from Upper Guinea. Moreover, during the same period, the tobacco-growing Chesapeake region drew on Upper Guinea to almost exactly the same degree as its lowcountry counterpart, while other North American regions received proportionately the largest share—just over half—of their slaves from Upper Guinea. In short, parts of North America other than the lowcountry have as good or an even better claim to be linked to rice-growing areas in Africa. In the first half of the eighteenth century, the relationship between the lowcountry and the rice growing region of West Africa was weak. . . .

Africans had a massive impact on the Atlantic world that went far beyond lives of unrelenting labor on American plantations. Like all migrants, both coerced and free, they carried knowledge of how to live, including how to produce, that helped make the societies of the Americas different from those of both Europe and, indeed, Africa. In lowcountry rice production, there is no question that some slaves introduced into the Americas a distinctively African sowing style, pressing a hole with the heel and covering the rice seed with the foot; that they hand-processed rice using an African-style mortar and pestle; and that they fanned rice with African-style coiled grass baskets. As slaves planted, hulled, and winnowed—accompanied by their distinctive songs—they incorporated African folkways into their routines. But these "survivals" do not amount to "an entire agricultural complex."

Furthermore, a close look at the slave trade from an Atlantic perspective suggests no evidence that the rice culture of South Carolina, Georgia, Amazonia, and Suriname was any more dependent on skills imported from Africa than were its tobacco and sugar counterparts in the Chesapeake, the Caribbean, and Brazil. The evolving transatlantic connections, the age and sex composition of the slave trade, the broad shifts over time in transatlantic slaving patterns, and the structure of slave prices are all largely explained without reference to a supposed desire on the part of rice planters for slaves with rice-growing expertise developed in Africa. Lowcountry rice cultivation would have followed a similar trajectory if the slave trade had drawn exclusively on Angola.

Interpretations such as those presented in *Black Rice* are drawn by tracking migrants from one side of the Atlantic to the other, and tracing cultural connections between the societies they left behind and the societies to which they subsequently contributed. Historians engaged in such an exercise are unlikely to conclude that such links are unimportant. More fundamentally, such an approach discourages giving due weight to influences that are unseen or that cannot be linked to the Old World roots of the group being studied. The New World environment—as much sociopolitical as ecological, for what was basically at issue is who had the power to transform the plantation economy and reorient it to new crops—contributed much to the development of risiculture in the Americas. Slaves arrived in the Americas with certain skills, perhaps the most important of which was their basic farming knowledge, and some of them contributed ideas about rice cultivation. Nevertheless, planters held the reins of power, had access to capital, experimented keenly, and in essence called the shots. A desire to celebrate an African accomplishment in the New World should not obscure the elementary power dynamics involved in the institution of slavery. Most important of all, a larger Atlantic economy and culture had enormous influence over those highly peripheral areas that concentrated on growing rice. Sugar ultimately set the terms for most other activities in the Americas.

For the most part, interpretations of the re-peopling of the New World continue to observe the old fault line that separates Old World cultural continuities from local environmental influences in the Americas. The "black rice" hypothesis belongs to the former, or folkways, end of this interpretive continuum. But in contrast to most studies that are similarly positioned, whether their subject is European free or African coerced transatlantic migration, the supporters of the "black rice" thesis cannot base their case on high-volume migration from the Old World culture that spawned the influence (Upper Guinea) to the New World society that it shaped (South Carolina and Amazonia). Rather, they must posit a charter-generation argument in which founding migrants have an influence out of all proportion to their numbers. The possibility of a single enslaved African women carrying a few grains of rice in her hair can become all that is necessary to sustain the thesis. Admittedly, there are some instances in Atlantic history—the Yoruba and Spanish come to mind—where specific diasporas probably had an influence on the Americas that belied the size of their respective migrant flows (in both relative and absolute terms). But in the case of the peoples from rice-growing areas of Africa taken to the early lowcountry and Amazonia, the numbers are so small, the gender composition so strongly male, and the alternative explanations for such a connection so numerous and persuasive that continued acceptance of the "black rice" argument is problematic. More broadly, a genuinely Atlantic perspective should integrate all forces—seen and unseen, relating to both inheritance and experience—into an account of the forging of communities and cultures in the Americas. Atlantic history was the result of the creolization of peoples from four continents. It was much more than the sum of particular bilateral transatlantic connections.

Eric Williams

Slavery, Industrialization, and Abolition

In his classic study *Capitalism and Slavery*, Eric Williams argues vigorously that the industrial revolution in Britain was closely linked to profits from the trade in African slaves. He includes in his calculations revenues from all parts of the "triangle trade" in the Atlantic—that is, from the trade of goods to Africa, from the Middle Passage, and from the sugar production in the Caribbean brought back to Europe. He further ties the British abolitionist effort to the rise of the new industrial class.

Britain was accumulating great wealth from the triangular trade. The increase of consumption goods called forth by that trade inevitably drew in its train the development of the productive power of the country. This industrial expansion required finance. What man in the first three-quarters of the eighteenth century was better able to afford the ready capital than a West Indian sugar planter or a Liverpool slave trader? . . . [A]bsentee planters purchased land in England, where they were able to use their wealth to finance the great developments associated with the Agricultural Revolution. . . . [T]he investment of profits from the triangular trade in British industry . . . supplied part of the huge outlay for the construction of the vast plants to meet the needs of the new productive process and the new markets. . . .

The triangular trade made an enormous contribution to Britain's industrial development. The profits from this trade fertilized the entire productive system of the country. . . . But it must not be inferred that the triangular trade was solely and entirely responsible for the economic development. The growth of the internal market in England, the ploughing-in of the profits from industry to generate still further capital and achieve still greater expansion, played a large part. But this industrial development, stimulated by mercantilism, later outgrew mercantilism and destroyed it.

In 1783 the shape of things to come was clearly visible. The steam engine's potentialities were not an academic question. Sixty-six engines were in operation, two-thirds of these in mines and foundries. Improved methods of coal mining, combined with the influence of steam, resulted in a great expansion of the iron industry. Production increased four times between 1740 and 1788, the number of furnaces rose by one-half. The iron bridge and the iron railroad had appeared; the Carron Works had been founded; and Wilkinson was already famous as "the father of the iron trade." Cotton, the queen of the Industrial Revolution, responded readily to the new inventions, unhampered as it was by the traditions and guild restrictions which impeded its older rival, wool. Laissez faire became a practice in the new industry long before it penetrated the text books as orthodox economic theory. The spinning jenny, the water frame, the mule, revolutionized the industry, which, as a result, showed a continuous upward trend. Between 1700 and 1780 imports of raw cotton increased more than three times, exports of cotton goods fifteen times. The population of Manchester increased by nearly one-half between 1757 and 1773, the numbers engaged in the cotton industry quadrupled between 1750 and 1785. Not only heavy industry, cotton, too—the two industries that were to dominate the period 1783–1850—was gathering strength for the assault on the system of monopoly which had for so long been deemed essential to the existence and prosperity of both.

The entire economy of England was stimulated by this beneficent breath of increased production. The output of the Staffordshire potteries increased fivefold in value between 1725 and 1777. The tonnage of shipping leaving English ports more than doubled between

1700 and 1781. English imports increased fourfold between 1715 and 1775, exports trebled between 1700 and 1771. English industry in 1783 was like Gulliver, tied down by the Lilliputian restrictions of mercantilism. . . .

In June, 1783, the Prime Minister, Lord North, complimented the Quaker opponents of the slave trade on their humanity, but regretted that its abolition was an impossibility, as the trade had become necessary to almost every nation in Europe. Slave traders and sugar planters rubbed their hands in glee. The West Indian colonies were still the darlings of the empire, the most precious jewels in the British diadem.

But the rumblings of the inevitable storm were audible for those who had ears to hear. The year of Yorktown was the year of Watt's second patent, that for the rotary motion, which converted the steam engine into a source of motive power and made industrial England, in Matthew Boulton's phrase, "steam-mill mad." Rodney's victory over the French, which saved the sugar colonies, coincided with Watt's utilization of the expansive power of steam to obtain the double stroke for his pistons. The peace treaty of 1783 was being signed while Henry Cort was working on his puddling process which revolutionized the iron industry. The stage was set for that gigantic development of British capitalism which upset the political structure of the country in 1832 and thereby made possible the attack on monopoly in general and West Indian monopoly in particular. . . .

The attack on the West Indians was more than an attack on slavery. It was an attack on monopoly. Their opponents were not only the humanitarians but the capitalists. The reason for the attack was not only that the West Indian economic system was vicious but that it was also so unprofitable that for this reason alone its destruction was inevitable. The agent for Jamaica complained in 1827 that "the cause of the colonies altogether, but more especially that part of it which touches upon property in slaves, is so unattractive to florid orators and so unpopular with the public, that we have and must have very little protection from Parliamentary speaking." Hibbert was only half right. If West Indian slavery was detestable, West Indian monopoly was unpopular, and the united odium of both was more than the colonies could bear.

The attack falls into three phases: the attack on the slave trade, the attack on slavery, the attack on the preferential sugar duties. The slave trade was abolished in 1807, slavery in 1833, the sugar preference in 1846. The three events are inseparable. The very vested interests which had been built up by the slave system now turned and destroyed that system. The humanitarians, in attacking the system in its weakest and most indefensible spot, spoke a language that the masses could understand. They could never have succeeded a hundred years before when every important capitalist interest was on the side of the colonial system. "It was an arduous hill to climb," sang Wordsworth in praise of Clarkson. The top would never have been reached but for the defection of the capitalists from the ranks of the slave-owners and slave traders. The West Indians, pampered and petted and spoiled for a century and a half, made the mistake of elevating into a law of nature what was actually only a law of mercantilism. They thought themselves indispensable and carried over to an age of anti-imperialism the lessons they had been taught in an age of commercial imperialism. When, to their surprise, the "invisible hand" of Adam Smith turned against them, they could turn only to the invisible hand of God. The rise and fall of mercantilism is the rise and fall of slavery. . . .

The strength of the British sugar islands before 1783 lay in the fact that as sugar producers they had few competitors. In so far as they could, they would permit none. They resisted the attempt to introduce the cultivation of sugar (and cotton) into Sierra Leone on the ground that it would be a precedent to "foreign nations, who have as yet no colonies anywhere," and might prove detrimental to those who possessed West Indian colonies; just as a century previously they had opposed the cultivation of indigo in Africa. Their chief competitors in the sugar trade were Brazil and the French islands, Cuba being hampered by the extreme exclusiveness of Spanish mercantilism. This situation was radically altered when Saint Domingue forged ahead in the years immediately following the secession of the mainland colonies. . . .

Whereas before, in the eighteenth century, every important vested interest in England was lined up on the side of monopoly and the colonial system; after 1783, one by one, every one of those interests came out against monopoly and the West Indian slave system. British exports to the world were in manufactured goods which could be paid for only in raw materials—the cotton of the United States, the cotton, coffee and sugar of Brazil, the sugar of Cuba, the sugar and cotton of India. The expansion of British exports depended on the capacity of Britain to absorb the raw material as payment. The British West Indian monopoly, prohibiting the importation of non-British-plantation sugar for home consumption, stood in the way. Every important vested interest—the cotton manufacturers, the shipowners, the sugar refiners; every important industrial and commercial town—London, Manchester, Liverpool, Birmingham, Sheffield, the West Riding of Yorkshire, joined in the attack on West Indian slavery and West Indian monopoly. The abolitionists, significantly, concentrated their attack on the industrial centers.

The West Indian planters in the eighteenth century were both exporters of raw cotton and importers of cotton manufactures. In both respects, as we have seen, they had become increasingly negligble. The steam engine and the cotton gin changed Manchester's indifference into downright hostility. As early as 1788 Wilberforce exulted at the fact that a liberal subscription towards abolition had been raised at Manchester, "deeply interested in the African trade." Manchester was unrepresented in the House of Commons before 1832, so its parliamentary denunciation of the West Indian system comes only after that date. . . .

As early as 1788 an abolition society was started in Birmingham and a liberal subscription collected for the cause. In this society the ironmasters were prominent. Three of the Lloyd family, with their banking interests as well, were on the committee. The dominant figure, however, was Samuel Garbett. Garbett was an outstanding figure of the Industrial Revolution, more reminiscent of the twentieth than the eighteenth century. In his breadth of vision, the scope of his activities, the multiplicity of his interests, he reminds us of Samuel Touchet. Like Touchet a partner in the spinning enterprise of Wyatt and Paul, Garbett was an associate of Roebuck's in the Carron Works, a shareholder with Boulton and Watt in the Albion Mills and in the copper mines of Cornwall. "There were indeed," writes Ashton, "few sides of the industrial and commercial life of his day that he did not touch." In addition his energy was thrown into the politics of industry rather than into the details of administration. He became the ironmaster's spokesman to the government. This was a dangerous man indeed to have as an opponent, for Garbett, in the larger sense, was Birmingham.

At a meeting of many respectable inhabitants of Birmingham on January 28, 1788, Samuel Garbett presiding, it was decided to send a petition to Parliament. The petition stated, *inter alia*, that, "as inhabitants of a manufacturing town and neighbourhood your petitioners have the commercial interests of this kingdom very deeply at heart; but cannot conceal their detestation of any commerce which always originates in violence, and too often terminates in cruelty." Gustavus Vasa, an African, visited Birmingham, and received a sympathetic welcome.

This was not to say that Birmingham was unanimous or single-minded on the issue of abolition. The manufacturers still interested in the slave trade held counter-meetings and sent counter-petitions to Parliament. But Samuel Garbett, the Lloyds and others of that caliber were, from the West Indian standpoint, on the wrong side of the fence. . . .

The capitalists had first encouraged West Indian slavery and then helped to destroy it. When British capitalism depended on the West Indies, they ignored slavery or defended it. When British capitalism found the West Indian monopoly a nuisance, they destroyed West Indian slavery as the first step in the destruction of West Indian monopoly. . . .

This study has deliberately subordinated the inhumanity of the slave system and the humanitarianism which destroyed that system. To disregard it completely, however, would be to commit a grave historical error and to ignore one of the greatest propaganda movements of all time. The humanitarians were the spearhead of the onslaught which destroyed the West Indian system and freed the Negro. But their importance has been seriously misunderstood and grossly exaggerated by men who have sacrificed scholarship to sentimentality and, like the scholastics of old, placed faith before reason and evidence. Professor Coupland, in an imaginary interview with Wilberforce, asks him: "What do you think, sir, is the primary significance of your work, the lesson of the abolition of the slave system?" The instant answer is: "It was God's work. It signifies the triumph of His will over human selfishness. It teaches that no obstacle of interest or prejudice is immovable by faith and prayer."

This misunderstanding springs, in part, from a deliberate attempt by contemporaries to present a distorted view of the abolitionist movement. When the slave trade was abolished in 1807, the bill included a phrase to the effect that the trade was "contrary to the principles of justice, humanity and sound policy." Lord Hawkesbury objected; in his opinion the words "justice and humanity" reflected on the slave traders. He therefore moved an amendment excluding those words. In so doing he confined the necessity of abolition solely to expediency. The Lord Chancellor protested. The amendment would take away the only ground on which the other powers could be asked to co-operate in abolition. The Earl of Lauderdale declared that the words omitted were the most essential in the bill. The omission would lend color to the suspicion in France that British abolition was dictated by the selfish motive that her colonies were well-stocked with Negroes. "How, in thus being supposed to make no sacrifice ourselves, could we call with any effect upon foreign powers to cooperate in the abolition?" The Lords voted for the original version.

The British humanitarians were a brilliant band. Clarkson personifies all the best in the humanitarianism of the age. One can appreciate even today his feelings when, in ruminating upon the subject of his prize-winning essay, he first awoke to the realization of the enormous injustice of slavery. Clarkson was an indefatigable worker, who conducted endless and dangerous researches into the conditions and consequences of the slave trade, a prolific pamphleteer whose history of the abolition movement is still a classic. His labors in the cause of justice to Africa were accomplished only at the cost of much personal discomfort, and imposed a severe strain on his scanty resources. In 1793 he wrote a letter to Josiah Wedgwood which contains some of the finest sentiments that motivated the humanitarians. He needed money and wished to sell two of his shares in the Sierra Leone Company, founded in 1791 to promote legitimate commerce with Africa. "But," he pointed out, "I should not chuse to permit anyone to become a purchaser, who would not be better pleased with the good resulting to Africa than from great commercial profits to himself; not that the latter may not be expected, but in case of a disappointment, I should wish his mind to be made easy by the assurance that he has been instrumental in introducing light and happiness into a country, where the mind was kept in darkness and the body nourished only for European chains." Too impetuous and enthusiastic for some of his colleagues, Clarkson was one of those friends of whom the Negro race has had unfortunately only too few.

David Brion Davis

Morality, Economics, and Abolition

David Brion Davis acknowledges the influence of Eric William's thesis in shaping the historical debates about British abolitionism. Davis uses the work of recent historians to demolish William's argument that the new industrial capitalists turned against West Indian slavery because it no longer served their needs, but proposes a different connection between industrialization and anti-slavery. By raising the status of skilled labor, he argues, the industrial revolution promoted an ideology of free labor that united British workers and employers in the crusade against slavery in the British Caribbean colonies.

. . . If we take a quick snapshot of Britain in the late eighteenth and early nineteenth centuries, it is not the first country we would choose in predicting the leader of a vast crusade to stamp out the slave trade and liberate hundreds of thousands or, through its influence, millions of slaves. Unlike the United States and France, England had no democratic revolution, and for British leaders the very ideal of equality was abhorrent. According to Edmund Burke and the anti-Jacobin coalition of Whigs and Tories, equality was synonymous with tyranny; aristocracy was synonymous with freedom in the sense of guarding against populist despotism and tyranny in the name of the majority. . . .

Despite some agitation in the 1780s and early 1790s for political reforms, especially the extension of suffrage, a powerful and prolonged reaction against the French Revolution, symbolized by its Reign of Terror, enabled a highly reactionary Tory government to block significant change. Even the modest enfranchisement of some of the more privileged middle class was not possible until 1832. Until 1875 some English workers were sent to prison for quitting a job. Antiquated "master-servant

From David Brion Davis, *Inhuman Bondage: The Rise and Fall of Slavery in the New World*, 2006, pp. 232–34, 240–43 245–49. Reprinted by permission of Oxford University Press.

laws" often required and enforced yearlong or even longer contracts between employers and employees, and the latter were often jailed for violating a contract. It is easy to understand why by the 1840s working-class radicals attacked and broke up meetings of abolitionists, who were accused of ignoring and diverting attention from nearby oppression that was far worse than the treatment of distant Negroes.

As it happened, despite reactionary politics and scenes of domestic oppression, Britain moved quickly from being the world's leading purchaser and transporter of African slaves to the total outlawing of its slave trade in 1807. Then, beginning in 1823, the nation took steps intended to protect and ameliorate the condition of slaves in its colonies in the West Indies, South Africa, and the Indian Ocean (but not India). And an act of Parliament in 1833 peacefully emancipated nearly eight hundred thousand slaves (who, as we shall see, were not truly freed until 1838), providing the then staggering sum of twenty million pounds sterling as compensation to the slaves' owners or the owners' creditors. In 1869 the great historian W.E.H. Lecky famously concluded his *History of European Morals* with the statement. "The unwearied, unostentatious, and inglorious crusade of England against slavery may probably be regarded as among the three or four perfectly virtuous acts recorded in the history of nations." Note that Lecky, no bleeding-heart sentimentalist, cautiously included a "probably"; for more significant, he was writing soon after the American Civil War had transformed much British opinion by freeing the largest number of slaves in the Western Hemisphere. Still, Lecky's phrase "perfectly virtuous acts" implies no hidden or ulterior motives even if England did very little to widen the opportunities for emancipated slaves and their descendants.

When dealing with an enigmatic subject of this kind, a subject about which we still have a great deal to learn, much can be initially learned by telling the story of successive efforts of some key historians to diagnose Britain's central interests and motives—what lay *behind* the abolitionists' success In "converting" the public and then the government of the most powerful and economically advanced nations in the world. . . .

In the mid-twentieth century, the most influential challenge to the humanitarian thesis came from Eric Williams's *Capitalism and Slavery*, published in 1944. Williams, a brilliant black Trinidadian, wrote a doctoral dissertation at Oxford, taught at Howard University in Washington, and eventually became prime minister of Trinidad/Tobago. His work is still widely accepted in the West Indies. During the 1984 sesquicentennial of British slave emancipation, his followers scorned any suggestion that Britain's slaves had been freed for humanitarian rather than for economic motives, despite the appearance of a growing body of scholarship that discredited Williams's economic arguments.

Williams's principal arguments support two broad conclusions. First, he maintained that European merchant capitalism created the immensely lucrative New World plantation system, fueled the Atlantic slave trade. According to Williams, profits from the slave trade or from the overseas slave system as a whole (it was sometimes difficult to tell which Williams meant) provided most of the capital that financed the English Industrial Revolution.

Williams's second conclusion stemmed from the assumption that the American War of Independence initiated a period of irreversible economic decline in the British Caribbean and also coincided with Britain's decisive shift from mercantilism toward the laissez-faire capitalism of Adam Smith. . . . Some earlier historians, especially Lowell Joseph Ragatz, in his *Fall of the Planter Class in the British West Indies*, argued that the period of irreversible decline started earlier, in 1763. Both Ragatz and Williams presented a picture of inefficient slave labor, white population loss, chronic indebtedness, soil exhaustion, and plantation bankruptcies.

Thus for Williams, these former island cornucopias of wealth were increasingly sustained only by mercantilist duties or subsidies that led to chronic overproduction for the protected British market. While Williams acknowledged that a "brilliant band" of abolitionists won fame by conducting what he termed one of the "greatest propaganda movements of all time," he argued that in the broadest terms, slavery was doomed by the transition from mercantile to industrial capitalism and free trade. . . .

It is Williams's second thesis, the one regarding the end of the British slave trade, followed by slave emancipation, that has provoked the most heated controversy and that is most relevant here. A succession of deeply researched works by Roger Anstey, Seymour Drescher, and David Eltis, to say nothing of a somewhat separate debate in which I myself have been involved, have reexamined the relationship between antislavery and capitalism.

In 1975 Anstey showed that by every canon of national economic interest, 1806–7 was the very worst time for Britain to abolish its slave trade. At that juncture in the Napoleonic Wars, Britain needed every export market outside of enemy control on which she could lay her hands. In the early nineteenth century, the British West Indies' share of Britain's total oceanic trade was *higher* than at any time in the eighteenth century.

In 1977 Seymour Drescher's hard-hitting book *Econocide: British Slavery in the Era of Abolition* argued that abolition of the slave trade was comparable to committing suicide for a major part of Britain's economy. Loaded with statistical tables and organized like a lawyer's brief, *Econocide* totally destroyed the widely accepted belief that the British slave system had declined in value before Parliament outlawed the slave trade. Using statistics on overseas trade, Drescher showed that the value of British West Indian exports to England and of imports in the West Indies from England increased sharply from the early 1780s to the end of the eighteenth century. Drescher also demonstrated that the British West Indies' share of the total British overseas trade rose to high peaks in the early nineteenth century and did not begin a long-range decline until well *after* Parliament deprived the colonies of fresh supplies of African labor.

After assessing the profitability of the slave trade, which brought rewards of around 10 percent on investment, and the increasing value of the British West Indies, Drescher contended that the British slave system was expanding, not declining, at the beginning of the nineteenth century. The 1807 abolition act came at a time when Britain not only led the world in plantation production but had the opportunity, thanks to naval power and the wartime conquests of Trinidad, Demerara, Berbice, and Essequibo, of nearly monopolizing the slave trade and gaining a preponderant share of the growing world market for sugar and coffee. Far from being "old" in some global sense — "old soil, old habits, old techniques," as Ragatz and Williams maintained — Drescher affirmed that "the British slave system was young . . . [and] it seemed so to contemporaries." As for the issue of soil exhaustion, complaints arose as early as the 1660s, and the erosion was never permanent. Plantation regions, like other farming regions, went through cycles of soil exhaustion and rejuvenation. . . .

Eltis's main arguments can be summarized as follows: Slave labor on the plantations of the New World and Indian Ocean (such as the British island, Mauritius) attained maximum economic importance after Britain and the United States had outlawed their overseas slave trades and during the half- century between 1816 and 1865. During this period Britain spent some twelve million pounds (a staggering sum) in its minimally successful effort to suppress the international slave traffic by patrolling African coasts, raiding African trading posts, bribing and coercing other nations to sign anti-slave-trade treaties, seizing suspected slave ships, and even sending cruisers to attack ships in Brazilian waters.

According to Eltis, slavery became more valuable to the Atlantic economy because economic growth created a soaring demand for such consumer goods as sugar, coffee, tobacco, and cotton textiles, all of which could be produced much more cheaply by slaves. In Britain alone, from 1785 to 1805, sugar consumption rose 80 percent and cotton imports quadrupled despite rising prices. The supposedly glutted markets of slave-produced goods that caught the attention of Ragatz and Williams were artificial and temporary. Britain's preeminent textile industry could not have survived without an expanding supply of cotton, almost all of which was produced by slaves until 1865. . . .

Having shattered the Williams tradition that antislavery succeeded because it advanced Britain's economic self-interest, Drescher addressed the quite different issue of explaining the power and immense public support of abolitionism. After rejecting economic interest as a motive, he emphasized the distinctive "political culture" that led a significant proportion of the British population to oppose slavery. By making informed comparisons with other countries, especially France, Drescher dramatized the remarkable uniqueness of the active British opposition to slavery, which cut across lines of class, party, and religion. This support, especially from the unenfranchised masses, cannot be explained by economic interest, at least in any conventional sense. Drescher argued that it depended on widespread literacy and a tradition of political consciousness and activism.

From the mid-eighteenth century on, publications like *Gentleman's Magazine* had attacked human slavery as a gross injustice; much English poetry conveyed the same message. The antislavery movement was itself a vehicle for political experience and training—for preparing men and women to form societies, to gather petitions, and to demand pledges from political candidates. By the late eighteenth century the British public not only refused to tolerate the intrusion into England of colonial institutions but began to insist that British standards of freedom be extended to the high seas and colonial plantations. From the colonial planters' viewpoint, this was "antislavery imperialism.". . .

But again, why was it England, a nation deeply transformed by the world's first industrialization and divided by class and religious struggles, that found a way of uniting a stable elite leadership with mass appeal— and in a cause that threatened specific property rights and social order, to say nothing of imperiling the economic benefits the David Eltis has so forcefully underscored? Whereas Drescher tends to idealize British traditions of liberty, Eltis says more about the continuing attempts in the seventeenth and much of the eighteenth century to ensure the industriousness of British workers by low wages and Draconian vagrancy laws. Such seemingly liberal notables as Bishop Berkeley, Francis Hutcheson, and Andrew Fletcher even advocated lifetime enslavement as the best means to discipline the beggars and idle rogues who roamed the eighteenth-century countryside.

Like Edmund Morgan, Eltis connects this early acceptance of coerced labor with a preindustrial preoccupation with competitive exports and low labor costs. As Robert J. Steinfeld has graphically shown, even through much of the nineteenth century British employers made frequent use of coercive, nonpecuniary master-servant laws to discipline and exploit supposedly free workers. By the late eighteenth century, however, an awareness of growing home or domestic markets was beginning to alert capitalists to the importance of "want creation" among consumers, as well as to such incentives as higher wages, as a way to increase both worker productivity and the number of consumers. Ironically, as Sidney W. Mintz points out in his insightful *Sweetness and Power: The Place of Sugar in Modern History*, it was slave-grown sugar that initially increased Britain's consumer-oriented market. . . .

The contradiction between the coerced labor used to produce plantation products and the consumer demand that eventually elevated British respect for wage labor sheds a wholly new light on Drescher's dichotomy between the metropolis in the British Isles and the colonial frontier in the Caribbean, Brazil, and the American South. It also brings us back to Eric Williams. In a statement that he unfortunately fails to develop, Eltis observes that

> the important aspects of the relationship between capitalism and abolition that Eric Williams was searching for were, first, that British employers had less need for coercion by the second half of the eighteenth century and that, second, both draconian vagrancy laws at home and predial [plantation] slavery in the colonies were examples of coercion. In the light of a. system that relied on voluntary labor to satisfy individual

wants going beyond subsistence needs, forced labor appeared not only inappropriate but counterproductive [since it limited the global consumer markets].

This reformulation of William's linkage of capitalism and antislavery asserts the importance of ideology—specifically, an ideology of free labor that would be understood in conflicting ways by workers and employers but that would nevertheless unite many of them in condemning chattel slavery in distant colonies.

In other words, by the late eighteenth century there was a pressing need felt by both skilled workers and employers to dignify and even ennoble wage labor, which for ages had been regarded with contempt. And what could better dignify and ennoble free labor, and even provide a sense of equality between the man who pays wages and the man who receives them, than a common crusade against chattel slavery? The very idea or image of chattel slavery, as embodied in countless pictures of slave ships and brutal masters, a whip in hand, lording it over semi-naked field hands, drew a boundary line that marked off what was now unacceptable, indeed intolerable. In the colonies and the American South, all labor, it was commonly said, was degraded by slavery.

Since Seymour Drescher's *Mighty Experiment* centers in part on "free labor ideology," it is important to recognize the difference between his use of the term and mine. He continually refers to the belief in the economic superiority of free labor. While I accept that meaning, I am more impressed by a deeper transformation in British and then American culture in the North: the desire to dignify and honor labor—a need and desire that made the British public in the early industrial era far more receptive to antislavery appeals. And like other ideologies, the commitment to free wage labor could be felt on a "gut level," apart from any explicit rational thinking. This kind of free-labor ideology conveyed a sense of self-worth created by dutiful work—a process that can cynically be seen as a way of disguising exploitation or can be viewed as a way of genuinely recognizing elements of equality in people of subordinate status.

I doubt that Williams's orthodox leftist followers would be satisfied by even a well-developed theory relating British antislavery to free-labor ideology, including the economic meaning conveyed by Drescher. Yet such a theory, based on more empirical evidence, would confirm some of Williams's most important insights: First, the slave system of the Americas contributed—both by the effects of its products on consumerism and by the imagery of seminaked laborers being driven by the whip—to *structural* transformations in British life that made abolitionism acceptable to almost everyone not employed by the West India lobby. Second, British leaders became committed to colonial labor reform only when they became convinced that free labor would be less dangerous than slavery and more beneficial for the imperial economy as a whole. (As we have seen, there were important second thoughts after plantation production plummeted and after Britain became infected, beginning in the mid-nineteenth century, by much pseudo-scientific racist thought.)

In contrast to Williams's cynicism, however, a theory based on free-labor ideology does not diminish the moral vision and accomplishments of the abolitionists. There is a world of difference between abolition as a calculated response to "overproduction," and abolition as a means of promoting and dignifying free labor. The laws of 1807, 1833, and 1838 show that, given a fortunate convergence of economic, political, and ideological circumstances, the world's first industrial nation *could* transcend narrow self-interest and achieve genuine reform—a reform that greatly improved and uplifted the lives of millions of blacks (counting later generations), that curbed some of the worst effects of early global capitalism, and that can well stand, as Lecky said, "as among the three or four perfectly virtuous acts recorded in the history of nations."

PART

VI Africans and Abolition

. . when He created the world, God Our Lord did not populate the earth with masters and slaves.

ALONSO DE SANDOVAL, S. J.

Equiano would appear to have been one of the abolition lobby's most persistent and convincing speakers.

ADRIAN HASTINGS

The white men . . . say the slave trade [is] bad . . . . [Why] did they think it good before?

OSEI BONSU, KING OF ASANTE

[If I] could do without slaves—it would be better for [me]; but . . . that [is] impossible.

EYO HONESTY II, KING OF CREEK TOWN, OLD CALABAR

147

The resistance of the slaves uniquivocally contributed . . . to the fact that the slave system was increasingly seen in Britain to be not only morally wrong and economically inefficient, but also politically unwise.

MICHAEL CRATON

Alonso de Sandoval

Questioning Slavery's Morality

Africans promoted abolitionism by the example of their sufferings, by participating in abolitionist movements, and by their rebellion. This essay by a Jesuit priest caring for newly arrived slaves in South America shows how the slave trade troubled observers in the early 1600s and how difficult it was to argue that slavery was immoral at that time. Father Alonso de Sandoval did not challenge the teaching of church authorities on the legitimacy of slavery, but his evidence and reflections speak for themselves.

The debate among scholars on how to justify the arduous and difficult business of slavery has perplexed me for a long time. I could have given up on explaining it and just ignored it in this book. However, I am determined to discuss it, although I will leave the final justification of slavery to legal and ecclesiastical authorities, especially the Jesuit Luis de Molina. I will only mention here what I have learned after many years of working in this ministry. The readers can formulate their own ideas on the justice of this issue. . . .

With regard to the blacks that come from Angola and so on, I have [good] information. These slaves might also be enslaved unjustly. I received a letter dated August 21, 1611, from Father Luis Brandão, rector of the college of our Company founded in San Pablo de Luanda. The letter says:

> . . . *Your Reverence wrote to me to find out if the blacks who come through Luanda to go on to Cartagena are justly enslaved. I do not*

Alonso de Sandoval, *Treatise on Slavery*, ed. and trans. by Nicole von Germeten, 2008, pp. 50–56. Reprinted by permission of Hackett Publishing Company, Inc. All rights reserved.

believe that Your Reverence should worry about this. In Lisbon, wise men of good conscience do not find slavery reprehensible. The bishops in São Tomé, in Cape Verde, and here in Luanda, wise and virtuous men, never argue against slavery. Jesuit fathers have been here for forty years, and there have always been learned Jesuit fathers in Brazil. None of us has ever considered this trade illicit. We and the Brazilian fathers buy slaves to serve us without feeling any guilt. When someone in Cartagena buys slaves, he buys them from a merchant in good faith, so he should feel no concern whatsoever. Here we should worry more, because we buy blacks from other blacks and from people who might have stolen them. But the merchants who take them from here do not know this, so they can buy them here and sell them there in good conscience. However, I know from experience that no black slave ever says that he deserved to be enslaved. Thus Your Reverence should not ask them how they were taken into captivity, because they will always say they were stolen or taken illegally, hoping that this will help them get their freedom. I would also argue that in some of the slave markets, some of the slaves for sale were stolen or their leaders commanded them to be sold for trivial reasons, so they do not deserve to be in captivity. But there are not many of these cases. Among the ten or twelve thousand blacks that leave from this port every year, it is impossible to find more than a few who were unjustly enslaved. Because so many souls are saved through enslavement, we serve God better if we save all those who were captured legitimately instead of not saving any of them for the sake of a few that were enslaved unjustly. The blacks are enslaved for many different reasons that abide by their laws and customs. Most of these reasons sufficiently justify their captivity. I cannot tell Your Reverence any more than this, because this is a very broad issue. Nor can I tell you about their rites and customs, because I do not have the time or health to do it.

Once, the captains of two slave ships coming from Angola consulted me on this issue, wanting me to help them understand if the slave trade was moral. They disagreed and wanted me to reassure them, so I listened and tried to help. One said: "Father, I go to Angola to buy blacks. This is a dangerous and expensive voyage. When I leave, after having spent a great deal on the slaves, I feel guilty. I ask myself, am I satisfied with how slavery is justified? The journey is very dangerous and costs a great deal in terms of time and labor. What if I bring them to live the rest of their lives in Christian lands, but they never become Christian?" I said to him, "Your trade is not immoral, and you will not be punished, because you say you bring the blacks here in good faith and for a good reason."

On another occasion a captain of a slave ship came to me very distressed because his fleet, carrying black slaves from Angola, was shipwrecked in a bay called Negrillos, not far from Cartagena. Only thirty out of nine hundred slaves survived. This story caused me great pain. The number of enslaved Angolans in the ships shocked me. I was also shocked by the reasons for why there were so many slaves in these ships. The rector Father Luis Brandão (whose letter we just quoted) had preached a sermon saying that some of the slaves were unjustly captured, so many of them had been set free. The captain of the ship explained why they had been captured, and his reasons were different from what the father preached. The captain said that two powerful kings were at war with each other. One sent his ambassador to us to enlist our help in bringing a great number of blacks as a gift. Although the gift of slaves included many good soldiers, the other king did not hide but took advantage of the gift. Then they both began a cruel war. The king who won was the one who had many slaves, as well as many captives from the losing side. All of these people were sold into slavery, which led to the huge number of slaves that came to Cartagena at this time.

There is a more standard way in which slaves are traded and later shipped in fleets of ships to the Indies. Near Luanda are some black merchants called *pumberos* [*pombeiros*] worth a thousand pesos. They travel inland eighty leagues, bringing porters with them who carry trade goods. They meet in great markets where merchants called *genses* gather together to sell slaves. The *genses* travel two or three hundred leagues to sell blacks from many different kingdoms to various merchants or *pumberos*. The *pumberos* buy the slaves and transport them to the coast. They must report to their masters how many died on the road. They do this by bringing back the hands of the dead, a stinking, horrific sight.

It is likely that many of the slaves that come from the Guinean rivers, especially Cacheu, a major slave-trading port, are enslaved illegally. When a merchant or ship owner comes to this port, they sell merchants their goods, normally printed cloth from India used for cloaks. They also sell wine, iron, and garlic to the Portuguese who live there, who are called *tangomaos*; in exchange for blacks. They also have agents, called carriers, whose job is to go inland with these goods to find blacks to exchange for the goods. This is how black slaves end up in Cacheu. In the Berber and Wolof ports, they sell prisoners of war or criminals. They fight wars over rumors and theft. The criminals who are sold into slavery have usually committed adultery, homicide, and theft. When someone commits these crimes, they bring together all the old men of the republic in the middle of the plaza. The criminal appears there, and they vote on the punishment, which could be death or, more commonly, captivity. The slaves remain at home working for the king or end up being sold on the coasts. . . .

A clergyman once went to Guinea in a fleet of slave ships. He went to investigate what he had heard about unjust wars in Guinea, the kings' power there, and black captivity. After he did his research, he said that there are no free blacks in Guinea, because all are slaves of the king. Here in the Americas a lord might own cattle and pigs in order to earn money on his farm. In Guinea the kings make a profit off of black slaves. With absolute power and dominion over them, they sell the slaves to anyone who wants to buy them. Thus there are no free blacks in Guinea—all are slaves.

I laughed heartily at this fantastic story, and I believed it deserved my laughter. But afterward, a document came into my hands that I will describe briefly, because it proves our point. This notarized document came from a court case here in Cartagena against a black man who came from Guinea and was trying to prove he was legally free. Although it could be proved that he was legally a slave, he could not prove his freedom. The case included a document that said that the king of Casamansa, as absolute lord of the Banhuns, commanded that this black man be sold into slavery as punishment for committing certain crimes. All Guinean kingdoms have the custom that when a black man commits a crime in his kingdom or another kingdom, even if he is a free man or a nobleman, the king can condemn him to perpetual servitude and slavery. All his relatives can also be punished by enslavement. This is not justice but absolute power. The king has the inviolable right to capture, buy, and sell as many slaves as he wants, even if the captured individuals are nobleman. Because the king commands it, all the slaves sold in his lands are legally enslaved and they remain slaves to those who buy them. They may never demand their liberty because no black are free if they are subjects of the king. Although this is completely unjust, this is what the witnesses said in this case. This evidence, along with the moral justifications argued by scholars, is the best we can do to carefully address this irredeemable situation and the very difficult business of the slave trade. . . .

We all know that when He created the world, God Our Lord did not populate the earth with masters and slaves, although clearly the Guinean kings mentioned above do not believe this. We also know that it was not until time passed and people became malicious that they began to tyrannize over the liberty of others. Solomon said that the poor man and the king, the monarch and the shepherd, were born with the same fate and under the same laws. In nature's forge, the prince and the plebian are crafted in the same way, and gentlemen are not born with more elegant clothes than peasants. Nobles do not have more eyes, feet, or arms than commoners. All of us live under the sky, the sun shines on us all, and we breathe the same air and endure the same elements. Both the king and the slave strive for liberty.

The Gospels of Mark and of Matthew say: Go all over the world, preach the Gospel to everyone regardless of lineage or condition, and make no distinctions among men. The Company of Jesus values a noble soul more than a noble body. We care more for a man's soul than for his status and fortune. God does not distinguish men in this way, nor should we so judge and measure them. True liberty comes from avoiding sin, and the greatest wealth comes from being virtuous. The redemption and blood of Christ, who bled for all of us, also equalizes us. A man's low condition and status do not prevent him from having value, nor does a grand lineage make him especially praiseworthy. Only faith matters, because slave and freeman are the same to Christ, and each one will receive a good or evil reward depending on what they have done in life. Servitude does not take this away, and liberty does not guarantee it, because both have the same importance to the Lord. There is no difference between the merits of a slave who serves well and those of a freedman who enjoys his liberty, because everyone should serve Christ. Servitude can be glorious, because God bought all of us equally with the blood of his holy son. All faithful workers, black or white, free or enslaved, have the same value.

Adrian Hastings

Black Abolitionists

The movement to end the slave trade began in Europe, not in Africa, but, as the following piece reminds us, Africans and African Americans played important roles in that movement. British historian Adrian Hastings explains the roles blacks played in the campaign that turned the British from being the Atlantic's biggest slave traders to being the slave trade's biggest opponents. Prominent among them was the former captive Olaudah Equiano.

On 19 March 1783 a young Christian Igbo in his late thirties called on Granville Sharp, the anti-slavery agitator, at his London home, to bring to his attention a report of how 130 Africans had been thrown into the sea off a slave-ship for the sake of the insurance money. The Igbo was Olaudah Equiano, and Sharp in consequence began another of his campaigns to bring the perpetrators to justice. He was not successful. It was the first recorded appearance of Equiano upon the public stage.

Captured by African traders from his home village at the age of 10 and sold to British traders, he was carried across the Atlantic, first to Barbados and then to Virginia. Here a British captain took a liking to the boy, bought him, and took him to England, renaming him Gustavus Vassa. He received some education, sailed in many ships, and acquired a good deal of experience of both the West Indies and North America. He was baptized while still a boy in 1759 and later had an experience of conviction of salvation by faith in Christ alone while on a ship in Cadiz harbour in 1774. His pocket Bible, he could write, "was my only companion and comfort." In 1779 he had applied to the Bishop of London to be ordained and sent as a missionary to Africa, but this petition was not accepted. In the following years he emerged as a leader of London Africans, a considerable little community, and active in the struggle against slavery. It was as such that he approached Sharp in the spring of 1783.

Adrian Hastings, "Abolitionists Black and White" from *The Church in Africa: 1450–1950*, 1994, pp. 173–175, 179–180, 182–184. Reprinted by permission of Oxford University Press.

(Left) "Am I Not a Man and a Brother?" Rhode Island Almanac, 1834. (Right) "Am I Not a Sister?" From the cover of The Liberty Almanac for 1851, published by the American and Foreign Anti-Slavery Society. (Both courtesy Library Company of Philadelphia)

One of Equiano's friends, Ottobah Cugoano, a Fanti with the English name of John Stuart, published in 1787 a book entitled *Thoughts and Sentiments on the Evils of Slavery.* It included the fiercest of denunciations of "abominable, mean, beastly, cruel, bloody slavery carried on by the inhuman, barbarous Europeans against the poor unfortunate Black Africans," "an injury and robbery contrary to all law, civilization, reason, justice, equity and charity." Writing in a Protestant country, the author appropriately insisted that "Protestants, as they are called, are the most barbarous slave-holders, there are none can equal the Scottish floggers and negroe-drivers, and the barbarous Dutch cruelties." This book was rapidly translated into French and appeared in Paris the following year.

Equiano and Cugoano were at once the intellectuals and the campaigners within the new African diaspora. It is true that there is some evidence that Cugoano's book may be the product in part of hands other than his own. One of them, indeed, may have been Equiano's. Two years later Equiano published a further book of his own which, while still being very much a piece of anti-slavery literature, was more naturally enthralling in being first and foremost an account of his life and adventures, including a quite lengthy description of his African childhood. There is no reason to think that Equiano did not write it.

Crowded slave deck, 1860. A U.S. Navy steamer captured the American ship *Wildfire* illegally carrying African slaves to Cuba. The slaves were freed and sent to Liberia. (Schomberg Center for Research in Black Culture, The New York Public Library/Art Resource, NY)

He was clearly a man of remarkable intelligence, versatility, and force-fulness, and his mastery of English is shown by letters surviving in his own hand. *The Interesting Narrative of the Life of Olaudah Equiano, or Gustavus Vassa,* as he entitled it, was indeed a very interesting book and it is not surprising that it went into eight British editions in his life-time and ten posthumously. But Equiano's considerable contribution to the anti-slavery battle was not confined to his books and discreet in-terventions with Granville Sharp. He was a campaigner all over Britain, for some years, travelling almost incessantly to speak and sell his book in the principal towns of the United Kingdom. Thus in 1791 he spent eight and a half months in Ireland, selling 1,900 copies of his narrative and being particularly well received in Belfast. The thought of this Igbo carrying on his campaign for the hearts and minds of the citizens of Birmingham, Manchester, and Sheffield in the late eighteenth century in favour (as he put it in a petition of 1788 addressed to the Queen) of "millions of my fellow African countrymen, who groan under the lash of tyranny" is as impressive as the book itself. Two points may especially be noted. The first is that it was not ineffective. Equiano died before Parliament declared the trade illegal in 1807 but it only did so because opinion in the country against the trade had steadily hardened, and Equiano would appear to have been one of the abolition lobby's most persistent and convincing public speakers. It is odd that his name does not appear in most accounts of the movement. The second is that Equi-ano represented at its most articulate a new social reality: a black, Prot-estant, English-speaking world which had grown up in the course of the eighteenth century on both sides of the Atlantic in the wake of the slave trade. A dozen of its leaders, "Sons of Africa," including Equiano and Cugoano, addressed a special memorial of thanks to Granville Sharp in December 1787. They had all been given, and willingly employed, European names, but it is noticeable that both Equiano and Cugoano chose to stress their African names on the title-pages of their published works, and Cugoano remarked insistently that "Christianity does not require that we should be deprived of our own personal name or the name of our ancestors." They had no problem in using both. . . .

There were at this time far more African Protestants west of the Atlantic than east of it, but it was appropriate that Equiano and Cugoano, the most vocal among them, should be based in London. London, one may well say, was not only the capital of the empire in which most of them lived (including, until the 1780s, the North American colonies), it was just at this point becoming a sort of capital of Africa itself. . . . No European state possessed more forts along the African coast; no nation carried in its ships more African slaves across the Atlantic; nowhere else in the world was there such knowledge or such concern for Africa, a concern demonstrated by the formal establishment in 1787 of the Committee for the abolition of the slave trade. It was essentially a British, and a London-centred movement. . . .

From the late 1780s Protestant Christianity would impinge upon Africa in a new and far more dynamic way. Granville Sharp, the charming, determined, but slightly eccentric protagonist of African freedom in London, was persuaded that it would be a real step forward if some of the black people in London, many of whom were penniless and in trouble, could be resettled on the coast of Africa. The "Black Poor" of London could be transformed into a flourishing, free agricultural community, an example of the way things could be without the slave trade. There was, in Sharp's vision, to be no governor. They would rule themselves according to the ancient Anglo-Saxon principles of the Frankpledge, as understood in eighteenth-century England. The government agreed to ship them out, and a first settlement was made in this "Province of Freedom" as Sharp liked to describe it, in 1787. The settlers were, for the most part, from among the dregs of London society with seventy white prostitutes thrown in, while the problems even a very well-managed enterprise was bound to encounter were huge. Unsurprisingly, it was not a success. Some of the settlers were quickly re-enslaved; some turned slavers; many died; quarrels with the local inhabitants mounted until in December 1789 a neighbouring ruler burnt the settlement down. Reinforcements, indeed a new start and a governor, were imperative if the whole exercise was not to be dramatically counter-productive: apparent proof of the inability of freed blacks to make good. A Sierra Leone Company was established and new settlers sought. At that point Sharp seems to have received a letter from Cugoano suggesting that there were plenty of suitable blacks in Canada, formerly British servicemen, who would like to go to Sierra Leone and might even pay their way: "They are consisting of Different Macanicks such as Carpenters, Smiths, Masons and farmers, this are the people that we have immediate use for in the

Province of freedom." Cugoano had been visited by Thomas Peters, a millwright, formerly a slave in North Carolina, then a sergeant in the Guides and Pioneers, now settled in Nova Scotia. Sharp met Peters, the director of the Company accepted the plan, and the Treasury agreed to cover the expenses of shipping. Thomas Clarkson, a leading abolitionist and a director of the Company, had a younger brother John, a navy lieutenant, who was willing to superintend the operation and did so very well. Fifteen ships were chartered to carry 1,100 emigrants from Halifax to Sierra Leone. In January 1792 they sailed; six weeks later they arrived in Freetown and the real history of Sierra Leone began. . . .

In 1807, however, a far more important development took place, the passing by the British Parliament of the bill for the abolition of the slave-trade, just twenty years after the Abolition Committee was first constituted in London and Cugoano's *Thoughts and Sentiments on the Evil of Slavery* had been published there. It was, despite the delay (in large part due to the counter-effect of the French Revolution and the war), an impressive achievement, going as it did against the undoubted economic interests of Britain and a powerful interested lobby of planters and merchants. It legally placed the interests of public morality above profit and market forces. It was in no way at the time a necessary achievement. It was managed by the combination of an efficient "moderate" leadership, at once religious and political, with a nation-wide public opinion produced by a great deal of campaigning. The sustained parliamentary spokesmanship of the morally impeccable Tory Wilberforce, personal friend for so many years of the Prime Minister, was invaluable, though the true architects of abolition were Granville Sharp and Thomas Clarkson, not Wilberforce. A cause which in the early 1780s still seemed eccentric was rendered respectable by the underlying support of the two greatest parliamentarians of the age—Pitt and Fox—and by its coherence with the best in contemporary thought, philosophical and religious. It would certainly not have been carried through without very powerful religious convictions at work which, starting from the Quakers, took hold of an exceptionally able group of upper-class Anglican Evangelicals, but it was by no means an inevitable consequence of the Evangelical Movement, and indeed its movers, Sharp and Clarkson, were far from typical Evangelicals. In America Evangelicalism brought no comparable conclusion. In Holland and France religion remained little affected by such concerns. Only in England did things take this course at the start of the nineteenth century, and it seems hard to deny that it was due to the persevering commitment to the abolitionist cause of a quite small group of men whose separate abilities and positions were knitted together to form a lobby of exceptional effectiveness.

Its effects upon Sierra Leone were to be momentous. The Act of Parliament sanctioned the stationing off the West African coast of ships of the Royal Navy charged with the interception of slavers. It was agreed that the cargo should be landed at Freetown, thus giving the tiny colony a new *raison d'être*. It badly needed one. The Sierra Leone Company's original aim of establishing a thriving settlement on the shores of Africa which would demonstrate by the success of legitimate commerce the economic pointlessness of the trade in slaves had wholly failed. The Company had never made any profits and its resources were exhausted. The British government had needed to subsidize it increasingly heavily just to keep Sierra Leone going at all. The unanticipated circumstances of a long war with France had destroyed any chance of realizing the original commercial aim, but there was, and long remained, only one really profitable trade on the West African coast and that was the slave trade, though a worthwhile timber trade was beginning to develop at this time. Inhabitants of Freetown, black as well as white, often abandoned the town, whose economy was negligible, to set up elsewhere along the coast as profit making slavers.

From 1 January 1808 Sierra Leone became a Crown Colony, the authority of the Company being taken over by Parliament. It had a mere 2,000 inhabitants, the survivors and offspring of various groups of settlers brought there from Britain, Canada, or the West Indies. Reformers and parliamentarians in England had thought little about the consequences of intercepting slave ships or what to do with their liberated cargo. They will not have imagined how many they soon would be. Certainly the blockade was far from fully effective; indeed the majority of slavers—in southern waters the vast majority—evaded capture, and the total number of slaves reaching the Americas in the first half of the nineteenth century was not so much less than the total number in the second half of the eighteenth. Not until the middle of the century was the trade effectively crippled, and only in 1864 was the last load of a captured ship landed in Freetown. Nevertheless, if many still got through, many were captured, and Sierra Leone was transformed as a result. By 1814 there were 10,000 "recaptives," Liberated Africans, in the colony, more than three-fifths of the total population. With the ending of the Napoleonic War the trade increased and recaptives reaching Sierra Leone could number 3,000 a year. The original idea that they be apprenticed to existing citizens or enlisted in the army could never work with many of the people arriving, women above all, but the numbers were anyway far too great. Subsidized for years by the British government, most inevitably settled, officially or unofficially, in villages beyond the town.

Osei Bonsu and Eyo Honesty II

African Opponents of Abolition

British moves to end the slave trade were not immediately welcomed by those Africans who had profited from selling slaves. In 1820, Osei Bonsu, king of the powerful Asante empire behind the Gold Coast, expressed puzzlement to British representative Joseph Dupuis at why Britain had suddenly ceased purchasing slaves, and also justified a king's role in selling slaves. Thirty years later, King Eyo Honesty II, the most powerful man in the trading communities known to Europeans as Old Calabar, voiced similar views to a Scottish missionary. Fully aware of the horrors of the strong preying on the weak, Eyo argued that the continuation of slavery was unavoidable.

A. Views of Osei Bonsu, 1820

"Now," said the king, after a pause, "I have another palaver, and you must help me to talk it. A long time ago the great king [of England] liked plenty of trade, more than now; then many ships came, and they bought ivory, gold, and slaves; but now he will not let the ships come

From Joseph Dupuis, *Journal of a Residence in Asantee* (London, 1824), pp. 162–164; from Hope Masterton Waddell, *Twenty-Nine Years in the West Indies and Central Africa* (London, 1863), p. 429.

as before, and the people buy gold and ivory only. This is what I have in my head, so now tell me truly, like a friend, why does the king do so?" "His majesty's question," I replied, "was connected with a great palaver, which my instructions did not authorise me to discuss. I had nothing to say regarding the slave trade." "I know that too," retorted the king; "because, if my master liked that trade, you would have told me so before. I only want to hear what you think as a friend: this is not like the other palavers." I was confessedly at a loss for an argument that might pass as a satisfactory reason, and the sequel proved that my doubts were not groundless. The king did not deem it plausible, that this obnoxious traffic should have been abolished from motives of humanity alone; neither would he admit that it lessened the number either of domestic or foreign wars.

Taking up one of my observations, he remarked, "the white men who go to council with your master, and pray to the great God for him, do not understand my country, or they would not say the slave trade was bad. But if they think it bad now, why did they think it good before. Is not your law an old law, the same as the Crammo [Muslim] law? Do you not both serve the same God, only you have different fashions and customs? Crammos are strong people in fetische, and they say the law is good, because the great God made the book; so they buy slaves, and teach them good things, which they knew not before. This makes every body love the Crammos, and they go every where up and down, and the people give them food when they want it. Then these men come all the way from the great water [the river Niger], and from Manding, and Dagomba, and Killinga; they stop and trade for slaves, and then go home. If the great king would like to restore this trade, it would be good for the white men and for me too, because Ashantee is a country for war, and the people are strong; so if you talk that palaver for me properly, in the white country, if you go there, I will give you plenty of gold, and I will make you richer than all the white men."

I urged the impossibility of the king's request, promising, however, to record his sentiments faithfully. "Well then," said the king,

> *you must put down in my master's book all I shall say, and then he will look to it, now he is my friend. And when he sees what is true, he will surely restore that trade. I cannot make war to catch slaves*

in the bush, like a thief. My ancestors never did so. But if I fight a king, and kill him when he is insolent, then certainly I must have his gold, and his slaves, and the people are mine too. Do not the white kings act like this? Because I hear the old men say, that before I conquered Fantee and killed the Braffoes and the kings, that white men came in great ships, and fought and killed many people; and then they took the gold and slaves to the white country: and sometimes they fought together. That is all the same as these black countries. The great God and the fetische made war for strong men every where, because then they can pay plenty of gold and proper sacrifice. When I fought Gaman, I did not make war for slaves, but because Dinkera (the king) sent me an arrogant message and killed my people, and refused to pay me gold as his father did. Then my fetische made me strong like my ancestors, and I killed Dinkera, and took his gold, and brought more than 20,000 slaves to Coomassy. Some of these people being bad men, I washed my stool in their blood for the fetische. But then some were good people, and these I sold or gave to my captains; many, moreover, died, because this country does not grow too much corn like Sarem, and what can I do? Unless I kill or sell them, they will grow strong and kill my people. Now you must tell my master that these slaves can work for him, and if he wants 10,000 he can have them. And if he wants fine handsome girls and women to give his captains, I can send him great numbers.

B. Views of Eyo Honesty II, 1850

The king maintained the utmost composure, paid respectful attention while we spoke, and then answered calmly in his own defence. He wished that he could do without slaves—it would be better for him; but, as the country stood, that was impossible. He did not employ men to steal slaves for him; nor would he knowingly buy those which were stolen. He bought them in the market, at market price, without being able to know how they were procured; and would let no man steal them from him. He admitted that they were obtained in various objectionable ways, and even expatiated on the subject. They came from different countries, and were sold for different reasons—some as prisoners of war, some for debt, some for breaking their country's laws, and some by great men, who hated them. The king of a town sells whom he dislikes or fears; his wives and children are sold in turn by his successor. A man inveigles his brother's children to his house, and sells them. The brother says nothing, but watches his opportunity, and sells the children of the other. He admitted that they were kidnapped also; but said that they came from different far countries, of which he knew nothing, and in which they had no other trade. Calabar people did not steal, but only bought, slaves. He concluded by saying, that he had so many, that his new people, if he did not protect them with a strong hand, would be constantly sold away again by the old ones, and reported to him as dead.

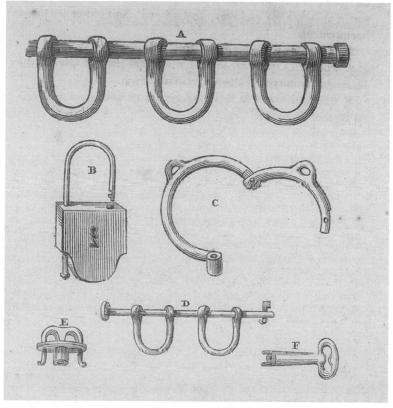

Shackles and padlocks used on slave ships in early 1800s. (Courtesy of the John Carter Brown Library at Brown University)

Michael Craton

Slave Revolts and the End of Slavery

Well before the first successes of the British abolitionists, a massive slave rebellion ended slavery (and the slave trade) in the largest plantation colony of the West Indies, France's Saint Domingue (modern Haiti). Profesor Emeritus Michael Craton of the University of Waterloo (Canada) picks up on this point, explaining how slave revolts in British Caribbean colonies affected the pace of emancipation. His conclusion supports a thesis offered by Eric Williams.

I believe it to be axiomatic that all slaves wanted their freedom—that is, freedom to make a life of their own—and that all slaves resisted slavery in the ways best open to them, actually rebelling, if rarely, when they could or had to. In rebelling, they seized the weapons that were to hand and used the aid of whatever allies they could find. . . .

Between [1816] and [1834], not only did the emancipation movement come to fruition, but there was also a crescendo of slave unrest in the British West Indies, with highlights in three of the largest ever slave rebellions, in Barbados in April 1816, in Demerara in August and September 1823 and in Jamaica between December 1831 and February 1832. What this paper aims to do is to examine each of these major outbreaks, briefly describing the sequence of events, the causes alleged at the time and what I take to be the truer causes, and the outcome, both in the colonies and, even more important, in the metropole. It will try to establish the relative parts the principal actors played in the drama of British slave emancipation, which was enacted barely a year after the suppression of the Jamaican rebellion; the avowed Emancipationists, the British legislators, the West Indian planters, the missionaries and, above all, the British West Indian slaves themselves. My main purpose is to test the conclusions by Eric Williams,

Michael Craton, "Slave Revolts and the End of Slavery" From *Out of Slavery: Abolition and After*, ed. by Jack Hayward, 1985 pp. 110–122, 123–126. Reprinted by permission of Taylor & Francis Group.

in 1944, that "the alternatives were clear: emancipation from above or emancipation from below," and of Richard Hart, in 1980, that British West Indian blacks were "slaves who abolished slavery."

The Barbados revolt began with thrilling suddenness on Easter Sunday night, 14 April 1816, at a time when the slaves were free from work and had ample opportunities to organise under the cover of the permitted festivities. What made the outbreak all the more shocking to the planters was that there had never been an actual slave rebellion in Barbados, and not even a plot had been uncovered to ruffle their complacency for 115 years. Indeed, so convinced were the Barbadian planters of their physical and psychological control over their slaves that they were certain that a rebellion could only have been generated by outside forces, namely the English Emancipationists, and fomented by local agents other than slaves, specifically a cabal of disaffected free coloureds under the leadership of one Joseph Pitt Washington Franklin, "a person of loose morals and abandoned habits, but superior to those with whom he intimately associated."

Some 20,000 slaves were involved, from more than seventy-five estates, and within a few hours they had taken control of the whole south-eastern quarter of the island. They fired the cane-trash houses as beacons and drove most of the Whites into Town, but did not commit widespread destruction or kill any of the hundreds of Whites virtually at their mercy. Having reached within sight of Bridgetown, they set up defensive positions, hoping and expecting the regime to negotiate.

They were soon disabused. Martial law was declared by the Acting Governor and the military commandant, Colonel Codd, was placed at the head of a punitive column. This consisted of regular troops, including the black First West India Regiment, and the much less disciplined and more vindictive white parochial militiamen. Codd encouraged the killing of all slaves who resisted and authorised the burning of houses and destruction of gardens, but still had to report that "Under the irritation of the Moment and exasperated at the atrocity of the Insurgents, some of the Militia of the Parishes in Insurrection were induced to use their Arms rather too indiscriminately in pursuit of the Fugitives." Whereas one white civilian and one black soldier were killed, at least fifty slaves died in the fighting and seventy more were summarily executed in the field. Another 300 were carried to Bridgetown for more leisurely trial, of whom 144 were in due course put to death and 132 deported.

Once the revolt was suppressed, the regime was at pains to excul-
pate itself. Whites asserted that slaves never gave bad treatment as a
cause of revolt, and masters were eager to demonstrate, against their
metropolitan critics, that Barbadian slaves were well fed, clothed and
housed, were not cruelly punished, received good medical treatment
and had opportunities to grow their own provisions and raise livestock,
even to sell their surpluses. The official Assembly Report, not published
until 1818, echoed the statement made by Colonel Codd as early as
25 April 1816:

> *The general opinion which has persuaded the minds of these misguided
> people since the proposed Introduction of the Registry Bill [is] that their
> Emancipation was decreed by the British Parliament. And the idea
> seems to have been conveyed by mischievous persons, and the indiscreet
> conversation of Individuals.*

However, such a spontaneous rebellion could not have occurred
without widespread disaffection, organisation and leadership among
the slaves themselves, and concerted, if unrealistic, aims. The [instiga-
tor] seems to have been a remarkable woman called Nanny Grigg, a
literate domestic from Simmons's estate. Nanny had been telling her
fellow slaves during 1815 that they were to be freed on New Year's Day.
She claimed to have read this in the newspapers and said that her master and the other planters were "very uneasy" about it. Accordingly, she
urged strike action, telling the other slaves "that they were all damned
fools to work, for that she would not, as freedom they were sure to get."
When the New Year came and went without emancipation, Nanny's
advice became more militant. "About a fortnight after New-year's Day,"
reported another slave, "she said the negroes were to be freed on Easter-
Monday, and the only way to get it was to fight for it, otherwise they
would not get it; and the way they were to do, was to set fire, as that was
the way they did in Saint Domingo."

Yet Nanny Grigg was no more than a firebrand. The real leaders
and organisers of the slaves were tightly-knit groups, cells, of elite creole slaves led by rangers—that is, slave drivers, chosen by the Whites
for apparent reliability, with much more freedom of movement than
most of their fellows. Chief of all these was Bussa, the ranger of Bailey's
estate, after whom the revolt has always been popularly known. What
motivated Bussa and his lieutenants, it seems, was a hatred of slavery

made intolerable by even worse than average conditions, coupled with a misguided sense that because the plantocracy now had enemies in England the time was opportune to rise up and dictate the terms under which the Blacks would continue to work on the sugar plantations.

What makes Bussa's revolt all the more poignant is the evidence that the rebels felt that they had the right to negotiate because they, even more than the Whites, were now true Barbadians. As Colonel Codd put it, "they maintained to me that the island belonged to them, and not to white Men." . . .

The chief miscalculations of the Barbadian rebels lay in underestimating the power of the local regime, in vainly presuming that the imperial troops would not be used against them (particularly the black West India Regiment), and in overestimating the support they might get from metropolitan liberals. In fact, even those in the metropolis who blamed the white Barbadians for bringing the rebellion on themselves by complacency and loose talk—calling slave registration but the thin end of a wedge leading to slave emancipation, and talking of imperial dictation over a Registry Act as tyranny worthy of rebellion in the style of the Americans in 1776—were horrified by the slave uprising. Not a single white person anywhere, it seems, reckoned the deaths of 264 rebel slaves as overkill.

[Abolitionist William] Wilberforce's own role was critical. Although he had supported the Corn Law in 1815 ostensibly in return for government support of the Slave Registry Bill, he was already wavering over the Bill before news of Bussa's revolt reached London at the end of May 1816. The news, though, seems to have convinced him that the Emancipationists had best "rest on their oars" for the moment. He did not oppose the address to the Prince Regent deploring the insurrection, and on 19 June made a speech so defensive and self-exculpatory that he came close to a rift with his brother-in-law, James Stephen. Clearly, Wilberforce was terrified by the thought that he might be held responsible for the Barbados slave revolt. . . .

Just as Bussa's revolt came in conjunction with the dissensions over the Slave Registry Bill, so the Demerara rebellion of August 1823 followed close on the heels of the next great wave of Emancipationist activity: T. F. Buxton's assumption of the leadership from the ailing William Wilberforce, the founding of the new Anti-Slavery Society in January 1823, Buxton's unsuccessful motion for gradual emancipation and Canning's canny substitution of an ameliorationist policy in May, and the Colonial Secretary, Lord Bathurst's first amelioration circular, which reached Georgetown on 7 July 1823. As happened in Barbados, the Guiana plantocracy angrily complained of imperial interference and dragged its feet over the implementation of the Bathurst circular. What further provoked the planters was that in British Guiana, unlike Barbados in 1816, nonconformist missionaries were already active and rapidly gaining converts, the most effective being the Rev. John Smith of the London Missionary Society, pastor of Bethel chapel on Le Resouvenir estate. . . .

Despite the planters' disclaimers, the Demerara slaves had even more cause to rebel than the Barbados slaves in 1816. Sugar monoculture had intensified and the slaves were worked harder and punished cruelly, callously shifted around with family ties ignored. Quamina, for example, on the day that Peggy, his wife of thirty years, lay dying, was refused leave to return to his house before sundown, when he found Peggy dead. For Christian slaves, the refusal of the planters to grant more than Sunday free from estate labour was particularly irksome, since it led to a conflict between the will to worship in chapel and the need to work provision grounds and go to market.

Christianity undoubtedly provided solace for many slaves, but less encouragement for rebellion. The missionaries, including Smith, were scrupulous in following their instructions to spurn political issues and counsel hard work and obedience. Bethel chapel was undoubtedly an important meeting place for slaves from the entire East Coast of Demerara, but subversive discussions occurred outside rather than inside the building. Likewise, Quamina, though a revered figure, seems to have been drawn into the rebellion rather than leading it, carrying no arms and being absent from the fighting. A far more dangerous type of rebel was his son, Jack Gladstone, a backslider in chapel but an ardent and wily agitator who was later to give evidence against Parson Smith and got off with deportation to St. Lucia.

As far as the Whites were concerned, the revolt broke out with shocking suddenness on Monday 18 August. Nearly all the 30,000 slaves on the sixty estates over a thirty-mile stretch east of Georgetown were involved. Again, by a concerted policy, there was little property damage, and the Whites held captive were merely placed in the slave punishment stocks. Governor Murray, himself a planter, on the first morning confronted a party of rebels and asked them what they wanted. "Our rights," he was told.

When Murray told them of the forthcoming Bathurst reforms, the rebels replied, in Murray's account, that "these things . . . were no comfort to them. God had made them of the same flesh and blood as the whites, that they were tired of being Slaves to them, that their good King had sent Orders that they should be free and they would not work any more." Murray then said that he would only negotiate once the rebels laid down their arms, at which the crowd grew ugly. Murray thereupon turned tail, galloped into Georgetown and ordered a general mobilisation.

The slaves were no match for the forces of the regime under Colonel Leahy, which, contrary to the slaves' wishful expectation, included well-drilled regulars, black and white, and Amerindians, as well as the local white militia. The only serious clash was at Bachelor's Adventure plantation, halfway down the coast, on 20 August, where 2000 slaves met with Leahy's 300 redcoats. "Some of the insurgents called out that they wanted lands and three days in the week for themselves, besides Sunday, and that they would not give up their arms till they were satisfied," wrote a militia rifleman. "They then said that they wanted their freedom," went another account, "that the King had sent it out—and that they *would* be free." Leahy did give the rebels three chances to lay down their arms, but when their leaders announced that "the negroes were determined to have nothing more or less than their freedom," and one prominent rebel waved a cutlass and dared the troops "to come on," Leahy gave the order to fire. The first volley scattered the rebels and in the ensuing orgy of hunting and shooting, particularly enjoyed by the militia, between 100 and 150 rebels were killed or wounded, at the cost of two wounded soldiers. The rest of the campaign was simply mopping up.

Besides the slaves killed in resistance, Leahy himself admitted that some sixty were shot out of hand, while an equal number were more ceremonially executed after military trials, a total of 250 slaves killed in all, compared with three Whites killed and a handful wounded. Quamina was hunted down and shot by Amerindians on 16 September, his body being hung in chains close to Bethel chapel, where it was left for months. Parson Smith was arrested and charged with complicity and incitement, tried under martial law, found guilty and condemned to death—with a recommendation for mercy—on 19 November. Suffering from galloping consumption, he died in his prison cell on 6 February 1824, a week before King George IV signed a reprieve with an order for deportation.

When the news of the Demerara revolt reached England in early October, it was a great disappointment for the Emancipationists but provided fresh ammunition for the pro-slavery lobby. Both sides were initially convinced that it was the timing of the Bathurst circular which had triggered the revolt, and even Zachary Macaulay went so far in attempting to reassure Buxton and Wilberforce as to maintain that the insurrection was "the work of Canning, Bathurst and Co. and not of your firm." Canning and the government duly reneged on their promise to impose the amelioration measures, except in Trinidad, and when Buxton opposed this in Parliament he felt himself to be "the most unpopular man in the House." . . .

The period between 1824 and 1832 saw a steadily widening gulf between the metropolis—Colonial Office, public and even Parliament—on the one hand, and the colonial plantocracies on the other. The Emancipationists, gaining confidence, made the crucial transition from gradualism to immediatism in May 1830, while, for their part, the colonial slaves increasingly took advantage of developing conditions. Slave unrest was wide-spread, almost endemic. Even in a non-plantation colony like the Bahamas, where the slaves were healthier, less hard worked and less supervised than elsewhere, dissatisfactions with slavery fed on rumours of imperial change. For example, the largest holding of Bahamian slaves, Lord Rolle's in Exuma Island, fearing a transfer to Trinidad and loss of their lifestyle, rose up early in 1830. A group of forty-four led by one Pompey, seized their master's boat and sailed to Nassau to lay their case before a governor, Carmichael Smyth, who enjoyed an exaggerated reputation for favouring slaves over their masters—being flogged for their rebellion but at least ensuring that they would not be moved from their island home.

Fittingly, though, it was in Jamaica—the richest and most populous plantation colony, with the harshest regime and most turbulent history of slave resistance—that the climactic and largest ever British slave revolt erupted around Christmas 1831. Jamaica was also the colony in which Christianity had most firmly taken root, a development that the planters regarded as chancy at best, highly dangerous at worst. Cautious proselytising by the established church or by the more "respectable" and regime-supporting sects—such as Moravians or Methodists—might usefully socialise the slaves. Yet the most ardent converts were the followers of "Native Baptist" preachers, who had originally come to Jamaica with the Loyalists in the 1780s, more than twenty-five years before the first white Baptist missionaries arrived in the colony. Obviously, the "brown Anabaptist priest" mentioned by Monk Lewis in 1816 was such a person. Another was Sam Sharpe, the pre-eminent leader of the 1831 rebellion, though he, like most of his kind, had more or less been subsumed into a white missionary's chapel as a deacon.

So many black deacons and their followers were to be involved in the Christmas rebellion that it was popularly known as the Baptist War — a fact that was initially a great embarrassment and only retrospectively useful to the white ministers who, like John Smith in 1823, were largely ignorant of what went on beyond their notice or understanding. From an extreme point of view, the preferred kind of "native" Christianity was quasi-millenarian, and thus politically explosive. Evidence garnered after the rebellion described "the rebel churchgoers' emphasis on membership and leadership, their fervent secret meetings, their use of dream, trance and oaths, their almost cabalistic reverence for the Holy Bible, [and] their choice of biblical texts stressing redemption, regeneration and apocalypse." Undoubtedly there was intrinsic tinder in the Native Baptist style, but a careful examination of the actions and aims of Sam Sharpe and his coterie of leaders suggests a close affinity to those of the vanguard led by Bussa in Barbados — who were, of course, not Christians — and that which included Jack Gladstone, Sandy and Telemachus in Demerara. The slaves' more or less authorised Sunday activities and the chapels provided cover for organisation and planning, chapel services contributed to rebel rhetoric and contact with missionaries even provided a sense that the slaves were linked with sympathetic allies overseas. But Christianity was not essential to the slaves' resistance.

Consider the best evidence of Sam Sharpe's activities in the latter part of 1831. Though he was a slave and based in Montego Bay, Sharpe was practically free to roam far inland on the pretext of preaching. A favourite meeting place was the home of a senior slave called Johnson (later to die at the head of an armed body of slaves some have called the Black Regiment), on Retrieve estate, a dozen miles up the Great River valley. One condemned rebel called Hylton later described how the charismatic Sharpe

> referred to the manifold evils and injustices of slavery: asserted the natural equality of man with regard to freedom . . . that because the King had made them free, or resolved upon it, the whites . . . were holding secret

meetings with the doors shut close . . . and had determined . . . to kill all the black men, and save all the women and children and keep them in slavery; and if the black men did not stand up for themselves, and take their freedom, the whites would put them at the muzzles of their guns and shoot them like pigeons.

The slaves, said Sharpe, should be ready to fight, but merely threaten force while engaging in strike action, binding "themselves by oath not to work after Christmas as slaves, but to assert their claim to freedom, and to be faithful to each other." A rebel slave called Rose testified that Sharpe asked him to take the oath. "I said Yes. The oath was if we should agree to sit down & I said Yes & so did every body in the house say Yes. Must not trouble anybody or raise any rebellion." Another rebel called Barrett testified that, "Sharpe said that we must sit down. We are free. Must not work again unless we got half pay. He took a Bible out of his pocket. Made me swear that I would not work again until we got half pay."

The Whites had some premonition of the drift of events as early as 15 December but largely ignored the signs, so that the uprising that began with the refusal of thousands of slaves to go back to work after the Christmas holiday ended on Tuesday 27 December, and the firing of Kensington estate high above Montego Bay that night, was a stunning shock. Almost immediately, the revolt spread over an area of 750 square miles centred on the Great River valley, involving more than 200 estates and perhaps 60,000 salves. The Whites, including a militia regiment defeated at a skirmish at Montpelier on 29 December, were driven into the coastal towns, and the rebels controlled the western interior of the island for nearly three weeks. Their hopes of bringing the regime to terms, with the imperial government as mediator and the imperial troops standing aside, turned out (as in 1816 and 1823) to be a cruel delusion. The Governor, Lord Belmore, promptly declared martial law, the military commander, General Sir Willoughby Cotton, acted with ruthless efficiency, while the white militia exacted savage retribution for their earlier setback.

This time, however, the regime's response was undoubtedly over-kill. Though the planters later claimed damages of over a million pounds (including the valuation of the slaves and the crops they had lost), no one computed the damage to the slaves whose huts and provision grounds were burned. Some 200 slaves were killed in the fighting (for less than a dozen killed by them), while no less than 340 were executed, including more than a hundred after civil trials once martial law was lifted on 5 February 1832. Beyond this, the local Whites, largely under the aegis of an Anglican organisation called the Colonial Church Union, carried out a veritable pogrom against the nonconformist missionaries and their congregations, burning down virtually every chapel in Western Jamaica. Sam Sharpe himself was one of the last to die, being hanged in Montego Bay on 23 May 1832; his last statement being, in the words of an admiring Methodist missionary, "I would rather die on yonder gallows than live in slavery."

. . . [T]he very day after Sam Sharpe's execution in distant Jamaica, [T. F.] Buxton made his crucial speech in the Commons pressing for the appointment of a select committee, not just a committee of inquiry like that of the Lords, but one that would "consider and report upon the Measures which it may be expedient to adopt for the purpose of effecting the Extinction of Slavery throughout the British Dominions, at the earliest period compatible with the safety of all Classes in the Colonies." Buxton's motion was defeated, by 136 to 90, but a committee was appointed, although with a mandate far short of discussing the means of emancipation. And the evidence that the committee heard over the next six months, in conjunction with the rising wave of anti-slavery agitation throughout the country, made it inevitable that the Whig government would be bound to pass an Emancipation Act within eighteen months. Key actors in this phase were the refugee missionaries, especially William Knibb (who, on hearing as his ship came up the Channel that the Reform Bill had passed, is alleged to have said, "Thank God! Now I will have slavery down!"); though another important witness was the same Rev. W. S. Austin who had been deported from Demerara eight years before.

Even the English public, it seems, was far more easily stirred up by the evidence of the persecution of white missionaries than by the slaughter of slave rebels—and in this sense the missionaries, as in 1823, stole the martyrs' crown. But the missionaries would not have had a case to make without the actions of the slaves, whether the rebels were their parishioners or not. As far as Parliament was concerned, however, neither slaughtered slaves nor missionaries tarred and feathered were as effective as the general threat posed to the imperial economy—to the empire itself—by the virtual civil war between the slaves and their masters.

The question for Parliament was essentially a political one; it was a matter of morality only in the sense that, in a liberal world, empire can only be maintained if its morality is justified. What Buxton was able to show in his great speech of 24 May, was that the actions of the slaves and the planters' counter attack showed up both slavery's immorality and its political impracticality. "Was it certain," asked Buxton,

> *that the colonies would remain to the country if we were resolved to re-tain slavery? . . . How was the government prepared to act, in case of a general insurrection of the negroes? . . . a war against people struggling for their rights would be the falsest position in which it was possible for England to be placed. And did the noble Lords think that the people out of doors would be content to see their resources exhausted for the purpose of resisting the inalienable rights of mankind?*

In perhaps his most brilliant and telling passage, Buxton then quoted Thomas Jefferson, a statesman by then universally respected but one of the most tortured of slavery's defenders. "A [slave] revolution is among possible events; the Almighty has no attributes which would side with us in [such a] struggle."

In sum, then, slave resistance and emancipationism were clearly intertwined in British slavery's final phase. News of slave resistance was disseminated more quickly, more widely and more thoroughly than ever before, while more and more slaves heard, if not always accurately, about Emancipationist activity in Britain. Moreover, slave resistance rose to a climax, in Jamaica, at the very point that the process was set in motion which led to the passing of the Emancipation Act on 31 July 1833. It remains to be decided, though, to what degree slave resistance and emancipationism, respectively, actually caused or speeded each other.

At the most obvious level, the Emancipation Act of 1833 was simply the political culmination of a widespread movement or campaign in the metropole. In conjunction with the general movement towards liberal reform, the small nucleus of convinced Emancipationists were able to carry the country towards a conviction that colonial slavery must be abolished. Through the interweaving of events—some of them, such as the victory of the Whigs and the passage of the Great Reform Bill, almost fortuitous—this popular conviction became translated into leg-islative fiat. This interpretation naturally plays down—if not actually denies—the effect of the actions of the slaves themselves in swaying first the British populace and then a sufficient majority in Parliament.

In an immediate sense, all the slave protests were certainly failures, and the slave rebellions of 1816 and 1823 actually set back the Emancipationist cause. Yet the slave resistance, not only rising to a crescendo but increasingly well publicised, gradually drove home the realisation both of the falsity of the assertion that the slaves were contented and of the plantocracy's claim to enjoy effective control. More than this, the increasingly paranoid behaviour of the colonial Whites both outraged and dismayed all levels of metropolitan opinion. . . .

At least some of the slave leaders . . . saw the political problems in its full dimensions. To achieve the aim of freedom, they realised, the slaves needed not only solidarity among themselves, but the strengthening of links with metropolitan allies against their immediate oppressors. Christianity was, at the least, a universalising medium, with the white missionaries as messengers and mediators; mediators not so much with God, or even that other Big Massa, the English king, but with the larger congregation of fellow Christians among the British populace. And, in the event, what was most impressive of all to this larger constituency (though the proslavery forces did their utmost to mask it) was that the rebel slaves, though resolute in their aims, were initially more pacific in their means than the plantocratic regimes which they confronted, only resorting to force . . . when met by actual force.

Thus, the resistance of the slaves unequivocally contributed—if not only in direct and obvious ways—to the fact that the slave system was increasingly seen in Britain to be not only morally wrong and economically inefficient, but also politically unwise. So, in assessing the contribution of the slaves themselves to the achievement of emancipation in 1833, one can conclude that while Richard Hart's 1980 claim that British West Indian blacks were "slaves who abolished slavery" is rather overstated, the earlier contention of Eric Williams that "the alternatives were clear: emancipation from above or emancipation from below" is much more than simply plausible.

Suggestions for Further Reading

General surveys of the Atlantic slave trade include James Walvin, *Atlas of Slavery* (2006); Michael A. Gomez, *Reversing Sail: A History of the African Diaspora* (2005); James A. Rawley and Stephen D. Behrendt, *The Transatlantic Slave Trade: A History*, rev. ed. (2005); David Eltis, *The Rise of African Slavery in the Americas* (2000); Herbert S. Klein, *The Atlantic Slave Trade* (1999); John Thornton, *Africa and Africans in the Making of the Atlantic World, 1400–1800* (1998); Robin Blackburn, *The Making of New World Slavery: From the Baroque to the Modern, 1492–1800* (1997); Hugh Thomas, *The Slave Trade: The Story of the Atlantic Slave Trade, 1440–1870* (1997); and Philip D. Curtin, *The Rise and Fall of the Plantation Complex: Essays in Atlantic History* (1990).

Collections of scholarship on slavery and the slave trade include Jeremy Black, ed., *The Atlantic Slave Trade*, 4 vols. (2006); Gad Heuman and James Walvin, eds., *The Slavery Reader* (2003); Stanley Engerman, Seymour Drescher, and Robert Paquette, eds., *Slavery* (2001); Patrick Manning, ed., *Slave Trades. 1500–1800: Globalization of Forced Labor* (1996); Joseph E. Inikori and Stanley L. Engerman, eds., *The Atlantic Slave Trade: Effects on Economies, Societies, and Peoples in Africa, the Americas, and Europe* (1992). The journal *Slavery and Abolition* publishes an annual bibliography of new works on the slave trade and slavery.

Investigating and understanding the trans-Atlantic slave trade have been dramatically transformed by the creation of a freely accessible database of nearly 35,000 slaving voyages at www.slavevoyages.org, which in its present form is the work of David Eltis, Stephen Behrendt, David Richardson, and Manolo Florentino. The site includes many introductory essays, maps, images, a guide to using the voyages database, and a separate database of African names. Eltis and Richardson have also edited a guide, *Extending the Frontiers: Essays on the New Transatlantic Slave Trade Database* (2008).

Studies of the circuit of Atlantic trade and the Middle Passage include Alexander X. Byrd, *Captives and Voyagers: Black Migrants across the Eighteenth-Century British Atlantic World* (2008): Saidiya Hartman, *Lose Your Mother: A Journey Along the Atlantic Slave Route* (2008); Marcus Rediker, *The Slave Ship: A Human History* (2007); Stephanie E. Smallwood, *Saltwater Slavery: A Middle Passage from Africa to American Diaspora* (2007); Emma Christopher, *Slave Ship Sailors and Their Captive Cargoes, 1730–1807* (2006); Robert Harms, *The Diligent: A Voyage through the Worlds of the Slave Trade* (2003); Bruce L. Mouser, ed., *A Slaving Voyage to Africa and Jamaica: The Log of the Sandown, 1793–1794* (2002).

The following works focus on the slave trade and its effects in Africa: David Northrup, *Africa's Discovery of Europe, 1450–1850*, 2nd ed. (2008); A. E. Afigbo, *The Abolition of the Slave Trade in Southeastern Nigeria, 1885–1950* (2006); Robin Law and Paul E. Lovejoy, eds., *The Biography of Mahommah Gardo Baquaqua: His Passage from Slavery to Freedom in Africa and America* (2003); George E. Brooks, *Eurafricans in Western Africa: Commerce, Social Status, Gender, and Religious Observance from the Sixteenth to the Eighteenth Century* (2001); Paul Lovejoy, *Transformations in Slavery*, 2nd ed. (2000); Robin Law, *The Slave Coast of West Africa* (1991); Patrick Manning, *Slavery and African Life: Occidental, Oriental, and African Slave Trades* (1990).

Books on ports involved in the slave trade include Stephen Behrendt, John Latham, and David Northrup, *The Diary of*

Antera Duke: An Eighteenth-Century African Slave Trader (2010); William St. Clair, *The Door of No Return: The History of Cape Coast Castle and the Atlantic Slave Trade* (2007); Robin Law, *Ouidah: The Social History of a West African Port, 1727–1892* (2004); James A. Rawley, *London, Metropolis of the Slave Trade* (2003); Ralph A. Austen and Jonathan Derrick, *Middlemen of the Cameroons Rivers: The Duala and their Hinterland, c. 1600–c. 1960* (1999); Franklin W. Knight and Peggy K. Liss, eds., *Atlantic Port Cities: Economy, Culture, and Society in the Atlantic World, 1650–1850* (1991).

African culture and identities in the New World are examined by Michael Gomez, *Black Crescent: The Experience and Legacy of African Muslims in the Americas* (2005); Gwendolyn Midlo Hall, *Slavery and African Ethnicities in the Americas: Restoring the Links* (2005); José C. Curto and Paul E. Lovejoy, eds., *Enslaving Connections: Changing Cultures of Africa and Brazil during the Era of Slavery* (2004); James H. Sweet, *Recreating Africa: Culture, Kinship, and Religion in the African-Portuguese World, 1441–1770* (2003); Linda Heywood, ed., *Central Africans and Cultural Transformations in the American Diaspora* (2002); Jane Landers, *Black Society in Spanish Florida* (1999); Ira Berlin, *Many Thousands Gone: The First Two Centuries of Slavery in North America* (1998); Michael Gomez, *Exchanging Our Country Marks: The Transformation of African Identities in the Colonial and Antebellum South* (1998); Philip D. Morgan, *Slave Counterpoint: Black Culture in the Eighteenth-Century Chesapeake and Lowcountry* (1998); Jane Landers, *Against the Odds: Free Blacks in the Slave Societies of the Americas* (1996); Sidney W. Mintz and Richard Price, *The Birth of African Culture: An Anthropological Perspective* (1992).

Guides to British abolitionism include Adam Hochschild, *Bury the Chains: Prophets and Rebels in the Fight to Free an Empire's Slaves* (2005); Seymour Drescher, *The Mighty Experiment: Free Labor versus Slavery in British Emancipation* (2002); and David Eltis, *Economic Growth and the Ending the Transatlantic Slave Trade* (1987). Drescher has also written *From*

Slavery to Freedom: Comparative Studies in the Rise and Fall of Atlantic Slavery (1999); and *Capitalism and Anti-Slavery: British Mobilization in Comparative Perspective* (1987). Recent works on the ending of the slave trade with a non-British focus include João Pedro Marques, *The Sounds of Silence: Nineteenth-Century Portugal and the Abolition of the Slave Trade* (2006); Laurent Dubois, *A Colony of Citizens: Revolution and Slave Emancipation in the French Caribbean, 1787–1804* (2004), and *Avengers of the New World: The Story of the Haitian Revolution* (2004); Sylviane A. Diouf, *Fighting Slave Trade: West African Strategies* (2003); and David P. Geggus, ed., *The Impact of the Haitian Revolution in the Atlantic World* (2001).